The Everyday Chef

FAST
& DELICIOUS

Published by Celebrity Press
An imprint of Hambleton-Hill Publishing, Inc.
Nashville, Tennessee 37218

Printed and bound in the United States of America

ISBN 1-58029-014-0

10 9 8 7 6 5 4 3 2 1

Graphic Design/Art Direction
John Laughlin

Contents

Conversion Table

Metric Conversions

1/8 teaspoon = .05 ml

1/4 teaspoon = 1 ml

1/2 teaspoon = 2 ml

1 teaspoon = 5 ml

1 tablespoon = 3 teaspoons = 15 ml

1/8 cup = 1 fluid ounce = 30 ml

1/4 cup = 2 fluid ounces = 60 ml

1/3 cup = 3 fluid ounces = 90 ml

1/2 cup = 4 fluid ounces = 120 ml

2/3 cup = 5 fluid ounces = 150 ml

3/4 cup = 6 fluid ounces = 180 ml

1 cup = 8 fluid ounces = 240 ml

2 cups = 1 pint = 480 ml

2 pints = 1 liter

1 quart = 1 liter

1/2 inch = 1.25 centimeters

1 inch = 2.5 centimeters

1 ounce = 30 grams

1 pound = 0.5 kilogram

Oven Temperatures

Fahrenheit	Celsius
250°F	120°C
275°F	140°C
300°F	150°C
325°F	160°C
350°F	180°C
375°F	190°C
400°F	200°C
425°F	220°C
450°F	230°C

Baking Dish Sizes

American	Metric
8-inch round baking dish	20-centimeter dish
9-inch round baking dish	23-centimeter dish
11 x 7 x 2-inch baking dish	28 x 18 x 4-centimeter dish
12 x 8 x 2-inch baking dish	30 x 19 x 5-centimeter dish
9 x 5 x 3-inch baking dish	23 x 13 x 6-centimeter dish
1 1/2-quart casserole	1.5-liter casserole
2-quart casserole	2-liter casserole

Salads

Baste
To brush (or spoon) cooking liquids over food
to prevent it from drying out.

Beat:
To mix ingredients until smooth by using a quick
stirring motion or an electric mixer.

Blue Cheese Pasta Salad

8 oz. pasta
4 oz. blue cheese, crumbled
2 c. walnuts, toasted and chopped
1 c. chopped celery
4 tbsp. mayonnaise
1/8 tsp. salt
1/8 tsp. white pepper
3 tbsp. minced parsley

Cook pasta according to directions. Immediately rinse with cold water and drain well. Add cheese, walnuts, celery, mayonnaise, salt, and pepper. Gently toss until the ingredients are well mixed. Refrigerate until ready to serve. If the salad seems dry, add a little more mayonnaise. Sprinkle with parsley and serve slightly chilled.

Note: This pasta salad is best when made the day before it is to be served, or at least several hours in advance, so that the flavor of the blue cheese has a chance to develop. Keep refrigerated.

Tortellini and Artichoke Pasta Salad

1 pkg. (10 oz.) cheese or chicken
   stuffed tortellini
4 whole marinated artichoke hearts
3 tbsp. diced roasted red pepper
4 tbsp. mayonnaise
1 tbsp. Dijon mustard
1 tbsp. grated Parmesan cheese
2 tbsp. chopped basil
2 tbsp. chopped parsley
salt and pepper

Cook tortellini; rinse and drain well. Toss with 1 tablespoon of the marinating liquid from the artichoke hearts to prevent pasta from clumping. More liquid may be added for flavoring, if desired.

Drain artichoke hearts and cut into chunks.

Combine all ingredients and toss gently in a large bowl to combine. Refrigerate if not served immediately.

Note: Canned, unmarinated artichoke hearts may also be used. In that case, use some olive oil to prevent the pasta from clumping.

If desired, add a little vinegar to give the salad some zip.

Romano Ramen Salad

2 pkgs. ramen noodles, chicken flavor
4 c. water
1/4 c. prepared Italian salad dressing
1/2 c. sliced mushrooms
1 green, yellow, or red bell pepper, sliced
1/4 c. black olives
2 medium fresh tomatoes, chopped
lettuce
shredded Romano cheese

Break ramen noodles into pieces. Cook noodles in water with flavor packets for 3 minutes. Drain and toss with all ingredients except cheese and lettuce. Serve on a bed of lettuce and garnish with cheese.

Marvelous Pasta Salad

1 pkg. macaroni shells
1 lb. cooked ham, diced
1 onion, diced
3 carrots, diced
1 c. canned corn
1 c. canned peas
2 sweet pickles, minced
1 stalk celery, diced
1/4 c. salad dressing (per serving)

Cook macaroni shells as directed on package. Combine ham, onion, carrots, corn, peas, pickles, and celery in large bowl. Add cooked macaroni shells. Mix thoroughly and place in refrigerator for 15 minutes. When ready to serve, add salad dressing to each individual serving. Note: Do not add salad dressing until ready to serve. If transporting this dish, carry dressing separately and add when ready to serve.

Shrimp and Pasta Salad

2 c. tri-colored spiral pasta
1 c. shrimp, cooked
1/3 c. diced green pepper
1/4 c. sliced carrots
1/2 c. sliced zucchini
1/3 c. white–wine Worcestershire sauce
1/3 c. mayonnaise
salt and pepper to taste

Prepare pasta according to package directions.

In a mixing bowl, combine pasta, shrimp, green pepper, carrots, and zucchini. Add Worcestershire, mayonnaise, salt, and pepper. Toss lightly to combine. Refrigerate at least 30 minutes before serving. Note: One can of tuna (6 1/2-oz.), drained and flaked, can be substituted for shrimp.

Oriental Seafood Pasta Salad

1 lb. medium pasta shells
2 cans (6 1/8 oz. each) white albacore tuna, packed in water, drained
1 pkg. (10 oz.) frozen peas, thawed
2 c. snow peas, blanched in boiling water for 30 seconds
3 stalks celery, halved lengthwise and sliced
1 can (8 oz.) water chestnuts, drained and chopped
1 tbsp. seafood seasoning
1/2 c. buttermilk
1/4 c. sour cream
1/4 c. mayonnaise
1/4 c. lime juice
1–4 drops hot sauce
salt and pepper to taste

Cook pasta according to package directions; drain. In a large mixing bowl, combine pasta, tuna, peas, snow peas, celery, and water chestnuts. In a small mixing bowl, mix together the remaining ingredients. Mix dressing with pasta mixture and stir to combine. Serve chilled.

Linguine Tuna Salad

7 oz. linguine, broken in half
1/4 c. lemon juice
1/4 c. vegetable oil
1/4 c. chopped green onions
2 tsp. sugar
1 tsp. Italian seasoning
1 tsp. seasoned salt
1 pkg. (10 oz.) frozen peas, thawed
1 can (12 1/2 oz.) tuna, drained
2 medium firm tomatoes, chopped

Cook linguine according to package directions; drain. In large bowl, combine lemon juice, oil, onions, sugar, Italian seasoning, and salt; mix well. Add hot linguine and toss. Add remaining ingredients; mix well. Cover; chill to blend flavors. Serve on lettuce leaves and garnish as desired. Makes 6 servings.

Tuna Macaroni Salad

2 c. (7 oz.) elbow macaroni, cooked
  and drained
1 can (6 1/8 oz.) tuna, drained and flaked
1 c. sliced celery
3/4 c. salad dressing
1/4 c. chopped green pepper
1/4 c. sliced green onions
2 tbsp. chopped pimiento
salt and pepper
lettuce

Mix macaroni, tuna, celery, salad dressing,
green pepper, onions, and pimiento. Season to
taste with salt and pepper. Refrigerate. Serve
on a bed of lettuce leaves. Makes 8 servings.

Macaroni Salad

12 oz. elbow macaroni, uncooked
3/4 c. plain, nonfat yogurt
1/4 c. mayonnaise
12 oz. smoked turkey, diced
2 celery sticks, diced
1 medium Granny Smith apple, diced
1 head lettuce, leaves separated, washed
  and drained
2 oz. blue cheese, crumbled

Prepare pasta according to package directions.
Drain and rinse with cold water. Put yogurt and
mayonnaise into a food processor or blender
and process until smooth. Set aside.

In a large bowl, stir together pasta, turkey,
celery, and apple. Add sauce and toss until
evenly coated. Cover a serving platter with
lettuce leaves and spoon pasta on to the leaves.
Sprinkle with blue cheese. Toss lightly and
serve.

Autumn Colors Salad

4 c. peeled, cubed sweet potatoes
1 apple, skin on, chopped
2 stalks celery, sliced
1 small red onion, chopped
1 tsp. fresh ginger, grated
rice vinegar to taste

Steam potatoes until soft, but not mushy. Toss all
ingredients lightly. Dress with vinegar to taste. Chill
before serving.

Carrot-Yogurt Salad

6 large carrots
1/4 c. olive oil
3 cloves garlic
2 tsp. salt
4 oz. plain yogurt

Peel carrots and grate them using a food processor.
Cook carrots in olive oil until they soften. (If
microwaving, use less oil.) Let cool. Mash garlic
with salt. Mix in a little yogurt, and then add garlic
mixture to carrots. Gradually add more yogurt to
the carrot mixture, mixing well after each addition.
Add more garlic and salt to taste, if desired.

Cabbage and Pineapple Salad

2 c. shredded cabbage
1 1/2 c. diced cucumbers
1 small onion, sliced thin
1 1/2 c. diced pineapple
5 tbsp. French dressing
lettuce
grated coconut

Combine cabbage, cucumbers, onion, and pineapple.
Add French dressing. Toss gently. Serve on a bed of
lettuce leaves. Top with coconut.

Oriental Cucumber Salad

1/2 cucumber, sliced thin
1/2 c. rice vinegar
1/2 tbsp. brown sugar
1/2 tbsp. water
1 tsp. soy sauce
1 tsp. sesame seeds
sesame oil

Combine all ingredients except cucumber in a medium glass jar. Seal jar and shake until blended. Refrigerate for at least 1 hour. When ready to serve, put cucumbers in individual bowls and pour dressing over them. Store any leftover dressing in the refrigerator.

Note: Do not substitute vinegars. The rice vinegar gives it just the right flavor.

Zucchini and Mushroom Salad

1 lb. button mushrooms
8 small to medium zucchini
1/4 c. wine vinegar
2 tbsp. olive oil
1 tsp. salt
2 sprigs fresh tarragon
1/4 c. water
1/4 c. dry white wine
finely chopped parsley

Clean mushrooms. Cut zucchini into 1-inch lengths. Place all ingredients except parsley into a pot. Simmer until zucchini are just tender. Turn off heat. Cover pot and let sit for 15 minutes. Drain vegetables into a bowl, reserving cooking liquid. Place liquid back in pot and cook until reduced to about 1/3 cup. Discard tarragon. Pour liquid over vegetables and lightly chill. Garnish with finely chopped parsley before serving.

Taco Salad

1 1/2 lb. hamburger
1 pkg. taco seasoning mix
3/4 c. water
1 head lettuce, broken into bite-sized pieces
4 medium tomatoes, diced
1 onion, diced
8 oz. cheddar cheese, shredded
1/2 c. sugar
1 bottle (8 oz.) Thousand Island dressing
1 pkg. taco-flavored corn chips, crushed

Brown hamburger; drain. Reserve 1 tablespoon of taco seasoning mix, and then add remainder to meat along with water. Simmer for a few minutes before removing from heat. Let cool. Layer lettuce, tomatoes, onion, meat, and cheese. Repeat layers until all vegetables, meat, and cheese are used. Refrigerate. Mix sugar, dressing, and reserved taco seasoning mix. Just before serving, add sauce and broken taco chips to remaining layered salad and toss.

Confetti Chicken Salad

1/4 c. fresh lime juice
3 tbsp. olive oil
1 clove garlic, crushed
1 tsp. chili powder
1/4 tsp. salt
2 c. chicken, cooked and cubed
1 red bell pepper, cut into thin strips
1/3 c. sliced green onions, including tops
2 tbsp. chopped fresh cilantro or parsley
2 jalapeño peppers, stemmed, seeded, and minced
3 c. cooked rice, cooled
2 avocados, seeded, peeled, and cut into chunks

Blend lime juice, oil, garlic, chili powder, and salt in large bowl. Add chicken, red pepper, onions, cilantro, and jalapeño peppers. Cover and refrigerate 2–3 hours. Add rice and avocado chunks. Toss lightly and serve.

Southwestern Grilled Chicken Salad

8 c. shredded lettuce
1 lb. boneless, skinless chicken breast halves,
    grilled and cut into strips
1 c. (4 oz.) Mexican-style shredded cheese
1/2 c. canned black beans, drained and rinsed
1/4 c. sliced green onions
1 large tomato, cut into wedges
Ranch dressing or salsa

On a large serving platter, form a bed of lettuce. Alternately layer chicken, cheese, beans, and onion. Garnish with tomato wedges. Serve with dressing or salsa on the side.

Chicken Caesar Salad

3 tbsp. olive oil
2 tbsp. Parmesan cheese, grated
2 tbsp. lemon juice
1 tbsp. water
1 tbsp. light sour cream
1 tsp. white Worcestershire sauce
1 tsp. Dijon mustard
1/2 tsp. anchovy paste or salt
1/4 tsp. pepper
2 cloves garlic, minced
4 c. Romaine lettuce, torn
1 c. fresh mushrooms, sliced
1 1/2 c. cooked chicken, shredded

In a small bowl, combine first ten ingredients to make dressing; blend well. In a large salad bowl, combine lettuce, mushrooms, and chicken; mix well. Add dressing to salad. Toss to coat and serve immediately.

Confetti-Rice Salad With Deviled Eggs

4 c. white rice, cooked and chilled
1 (12 oz.) seedless English cucumber, diced
1 large tomato, halved, seeded, and diced
1 large yellow, red, or green bell pepper, diced
1/3 c. red onion, finely chopped
1/2 c. bottled Ranch dressing
1/4 c. fresh dill, snipped
1 tsp. salt
1/2 tsp. pepper
lettuce leaves
Deviled Eggs (recipe follows)

Put rice and vegetables in a large bowl. Add bottled dressing, dill, salt, and pepper; toss to mix and coat. Serve or cover and refrigerate for up to 1 day.

When ready to serve, line a 2-quart serving bowl with lettuce leaves. Top with rice mixture and surround with deviled eggs.

Deviled Eggs
8 large eggs
2 1/2 tbsp. mayonnaise
2 tsp. Dijon mustard
1/4 tsp. ground white pepper

Hard boil eggs. Let cool, then cut in half lengthwise. Carefully remove yolks to a small bowl or food processor. Add mayonnaise and mustard to yolks. Mash or process until smooth.

Season with white pepper. Spoon or pipe into egg whites.

Steak and Onion Salad With Creamy Buttermilk Dressing

1/2 c. buttermilk

1 tbsp. reduced-fat mayonnaise

2 tsp. cider vinegar

1/2 tsp. coarsely ground black pepper

1/4 tsp. salt

cooking spray

1 large red onion, sliced thin

8 oz. boneless top-round steak
  (about 3/4-inch thick)

salt and pepper to taste

2 large ripe tomatoes, cut into bite-sized
  pieces (3 c.)

1 medium cucumber, quartered and
  sliced thin (1 1/2 c.)

10 c. salad greens, torn into bite-sized pieces

In a small bowl, whisk buttermilk, mayonnaise, vinegar, pepper, and salt until blended and smooth.

Spray a large nonstick skillet with cooking spray. Heat over medium-high heat. Add onion slices. Cover and cook 6 to 8 minutes, stirring occasionally, until lightly browned and tender-crisp. Remove from skillet.

Spray skillet with cooking spray again. Add steak and cook over medium-high heat to desired doneness, turning once. Remove steak from skillet and slice thin. Sprinkle slices with salt and pepper to taste.

Toss tomatoes, cucumbers, and salad greens in a large salad bowl. Add steak and onions. Serve with dressing on the side.

Chicken and Summer Squash Salad

4 8-oz. zucchini or yellow summer squash,
  cut lengthwise into 1/2-inch slabs

2 red onions, cut into 1/2-inch slices

cooking spray

4 chicken breast halves

1/3 c. bottled fat-free herb vinaigrette dressing

1 jar (2 oz.) diced pimientos, drained

5 c. Romaine lettuce, loosely packed
  and coarsely shredded

Lightly coat squash and onions with cooking spray. Grill 4 inches from heat source for 3-4 minutes per side or until tender. Grill chicken breast halves, then cut into bite-sized strips.

Cut grilled zucchini into rounds 1-inch thick. Separate grilled onion slices into rings.

Whirl vinaigrette and pimientos in a blender or food processor until smooth. Pour into large serving bowl. Add grilled zucchini rounds, lettuce, chicken strips, and grilled onion rings. Toss gently to coat.

Italian-Style Chicken Salad

2 jars (6 oz. ea.) marinated artichoke hearts

4 grilled chicken breast halves, cut into
  bite-sized pieces

6 c. bite-sized pieces romaine lettuce

2 jars (6 oz. ea.) roasted red peppers,
  drained and cut into bite-sized pieces

1 c. celery, chopped

1/2 tsp. salt

1/2 tsp. pepper

Pour artichoke hearts and marinade into a large serving bowl. Cut artichoke hearts in half. Add remaining ingredients. Toss to mix.

Pretzel Salad

2 c. pretzels, crushed
1 c. plus 3 tsp. sugar
3/4 c. butter, melted
1 pkg. (8 oz.) cream cheese, softened
1 c. frozen dessert topping, thawed
1 large box strawberry gelatin
2 c. boiling water
2 boxes (10 oz. ea.) frozen strawberries

Mix pretzels, 3 teaspoons sugar, and butter; spread in 13x9-inch pan. Bake 8 minutes at 400°F. Let cool.

Beat 1 cup sugar into cream cheese; stir in dessert topping. Spread mixture over pretzel crust and let cool.

Dissolve gelatin in boiling water; stir in strawberries. Let stand 10 minutes. Pour over cheese mixture and chill until ready to serve.

Mexican Chef's Salad

1 tbsp. vegetable oil
1 lb. boneless chicken, diced
1 lb. kidney beans, drained
1/2 tsp. salt
1 tsp. chili powder
1 medium onion, chopped
3 medium tomatoes, diced
1 lb. iceberg lettuce, chopped (about half
   of a large head)
1/4 lb. cheddar cheese, grated
1 c. Thousand Island dressing
1/4 c. picante sauce
1 large avocado, sliced
3/4 lb. corn tortilla chips, crushed into flakes

Heat oil in a large frying pan until it starts to smoke. Add chicken cubes and fry over medium-high heat, stirring frequently, until browned (about 2 or 3 minutes). Add kidney beans, salt, and chili powder. Reduce heat and simmer 10 minutes.

Toss together onion, tomatoes, lettuce, cheese, salad dressing, and picante sauce. Add avocado and tortilla chips. Mix chicken-bean mixture into cold salad. Garnish with extra tortilla chips and slices of avocado and tomato. Serve immediately.

Minestrone Salad With Garlic-Cheese Dressing

8 c. cooked pasta shapes (1 lb. dried pasta)
1 can (16 oz.) garbanzo beans, rinsed and drained
1 can (16 oz.) kidney beans, rinsed and drained
1 red bell pepper, seeded and diced
1 green bell pepper, seeded and diced
3 ribs celery, sliced
6 oz. summer squash or zucchini, diced
6 oz. small green beans
3 oz. Genoa or hard salami, diced
4 oz. provolone cheese, diced
Garlic-Cheese Dressing (recipe follows)
2 tomatoes, cut into wedges
shredded spinach or lettuce

Combine first ten ingredients in a large bowl. Pour dressing over salad; garnish with tomato wedges. Serve over shredded spinach or lettuce.

Garlic-Cheese Dressing

1 clove garlic
1 oz. Parmesan cheese
1/2 c. packed fresh basil leaves
2/3 c. olive oil
1/4 c. red wine vinegar
salt and crushed red pepper flakes to taste

Mince garlic in a food processor. Add cheese and basil; process until fine. Add oil, vinegar, salt, and pepper flakes; mix well.

Smoked Turkey Salad

1/4 c. mayonnaise

1 1/2 tsp. fresh ginger root, grated

1/4 tsp. curry powder

1 navel orange, peeled, white membrane
    removed, cut into sections

1 c. celery, sliced

2 tbsp. red onion, diced

2 tbsp. almonds, toasted and slivered

1/4 c. golden raisins

8 oz. smoked turkey, cut into 1/4-inch strips

4 slices pumpernickel bread

1/2 c. spinach, coarsely shredded

Mix mayonnaise, ginger, and curry powder in a
large bowl until blended. Add orange, celery,
onion, almonds, raisins, and turkey. Stir to mix.
Pile onto pumpernickel slices and top with
spinach. Serve open-faced.

Tuna and White Bean Salad

2 cans (6 1/8 oz. ea.) light tuna in olive oil

2 tbsp. red-wine vinegar

1/2 tsp. garlic, minced

2 tsp. fresh thyme, chopped or 1/2 tsp.
    dried thyme

1/2 tsp. salt

1/2 tsp. pepper

2 cans (15 oz. ea.) white beans,
    rinsed and drained

1 large red bell pepper, seeded and cut into
    1/2-inch pieces

Drain oil from tuna, reserving 2 tablespoons.
Pour reserved oil into a large bowl. Whisk in
vinegar, garlic, thyme, salt, and pepper. Break
tuna into large chunks. Add tuna and remaining
ingredients to bowl. Toss gently to mix.

Cobb Salad

1 small head Romaine lettuce, chopped into
    bite-sized pieces (12 c.)

1 bunch watercress, torn into small sprigs (4 c.)

3 medium ripe tomatoes, cut into small pieces

1/2 c. bottled Dijon vinaigrette dressing

1 can (11 oz.) vacuum-packed corn,
    drained (1 1/2 c.)

8 oz. cooked turkey, torn into 1 1/2-inch
    pieces (2 c.)

1 ripe avocado, halved, seeded, cut into chunks

4 hard boiled eggs, chopped

4 strips bacon, fried crisp and drained
    on paper towels

2 oz. blue cheese, crumbled (1/2 c.)

Arrange lettuce and watercress on 6 individual
plates. Toss tomatoes with 1 tablespoon dressing.
Toss corn with another tablespoon dressing. Place
tomatoes and corn on lettuce. Arrange turkey,
avocado, and eggs on lettuce. Crumble bacon over
turkey and blue cheese over avocado and egg.
Serve with remaining dressing.

Turkey-Mango Salad

1/2 tsp. lime peel, freshly grated

1/4 c. lime juice

2 tbsp. vegetable oil

1 tbsp. honey

1 1/2 tsp. fresh ginger root, grated

1/2 tsp. salt

1/8 tsp. ground red pepper (cayenne)

3 c. turkey, roasted and diced

1 mango, halved and diced

1 c. strawberries, hulled and quartered

2 scallions, sliced diagonally

2 c. spinach, shredded

2 c. iceberg lettuce, shredded

small spinach leaves for garnish

Whisk first 7 ingredients in a large bowl until
blended. Add turkey, mango, strawberries, and
scallions. Stir to coat. Add shredded spinach and
lettuce. Toss to mix. Line platter or individual plates
with spinach leaves. Top with turkey mixture.

Chicken and Cucumber Pasta Salad

1 c. uncooked macaroni
3/4 c. mayonnaise
1 tbsp. onion, chopped fine
1/2 tsp. salt
1/4 tsp. pepper
1 1/2 c. chicken, cooked and chopped
1 c. cucumber, chopped

Cook macaroni according to package directions; rinse and drain. In a large bowl, combine mayonnaise, onion, salt, and pepper; mix well. Add macaroni, chicken, and cucumber; mix gently. Cover and chill for at least 2 hours.

Bean and Pasta Salad

1/2 lb. small, hollow pasta
olive oil
1 1/2 c. white kidney beans or other
   small white beans, cooked
1 small red onion, sliced thin
1 stalk celery, sliced
2 small tomatoes, cut into wedges
1/2 c. small black olives
Dressing (recipe follows)
salt and pepper to taste
fresh oregano leaves for garnish

Cook pasta in boiling salted water until *al dente*. Drain, rinse under cold water, and drain again. Transfer to a large serving bowl. Stir a small amount of oil through pasta to prevent sticking. Let cool. Add beans, onion, celery, tomatoes, and olives.

Pour dressing on salad and toss thoroughly. Season to taste with salt and pepper. Cover and chill. Before serving, toss again lightly and garnish with oregano leaves.

Dressing

1/2 c. extra-virgin olive oil
2 tsp. Dijon mustard
juice of 1 lemon
1 tbsp. fresh oregano or parsley,
   finely chopped
salt and pepper
1 clove garlic, crushed

Combine all ingredients in a jar and shake well.

Awesome Spinach Salad

1 bunch raw spinach, washed and torn into
   small pieces
bean sprouts
Parmesan cheese
bacon bits
Dressing (recipe follows)

Put bean sprouts in a bowl over spinach. Sprinkle with Parmesan and bacon bits. Serve with dressing.

Dressing

1/2 c. fresh lemon juice
1/2 c. oil
2 cloves garlic, minced
2 tbsp. Dijon mustard
5 tbsp. Parmesan cheese
dash salt
dash pepper
3 dashes Worcestershire sauce

Combine all ingredients in a plastic shaker bottle and shake. Refrigerate for at least 1 hour.

Chicken & Seafood

Broil:
To cook food directly below the heat source.

Brush:
To use a pastry brush to apply a liquid to a food (e.g., a glaze).

Roasted Chicken Stew

3 qt. mixed vegetables (potatoes, carrots,
　　onions, celery)
2 tbsp. balsamic vinegar
3 tsp. tarragon, divided
1 tsp. thyme, divided
1/2 tsp. minced garlic
1/2 tsp. salt
1/2 tsp. black pepper
1/8 tsp. cayenne pepper
1 c. fresh green beans, cut into 2-inch pieces
3/4 c. dry white wine
1 1/2 lb. boneless, skinless chicken breasts,
　　cut into 2-inch pieces
2 cans (13 3/4 oz. ea.) low-sodium
　　chicken broth
3 tbsp. flour
1/2 cup water

Coat a large soup pot with cooking spray.
Heat pot over medium heat. Add all vegetables
except green beans, vinegar, 2 teaspoons
tarragon, 1/2 teaspoon thyme, garlic, salt,
and peppers; toss to coat.

Cook and stir until vegetables begin to
caramelize, about 30 minutes. Add green beans
and cook until vegetables are tender, about 10
minutes longer.

Remove vegetables to a large bowl and cover
to keep warm.

Add wine to pot and scrape brown bits
off bottom of pan. Add chicken and cook
until done.

Remove chicken to same bowl as vegetables and
cover to keep warm.

Add broth to pot and bring to a simmer. Mix flour
and water, stirring until smooth. Add to broth,
stirring until smooth.

Add remaining tarragon and thyme. Add chicken
and vegetables, tossing to coat. Heat until hot.

Skillet Herb–Roasted Chicken

2 tbsp. all-purpose flour
1/4 tsp. ground sage
1/4 tsp. dried thyme leaves, crushed
4 skinless, boneless chicken breast halves, or
　　8 skinless, boneless chicken thighs (about 1 lb.)
2 tbsp. butter
1 can (10 3/4 oz.) cream of chicken soup
1/2 c. water
4 c. rice, cooked and hot

Mix flour, sage, and thyme on a plate. Coat chicken
with flour mixture. In medium skillet over medium
heat, melt butter.

Add chicken and cook 15 minutes or until chicken is
browned and no longer pink. Remove and keep
warm. Add soup and water to skillet.

Reduce heat to low and heat through. Serve over
chicken with rice.

VARIATION: Add 2 cups sliced mushrooms (about
6 ounces) or sliced shiitake mushrooms (about 4
ounces) with soup. Substitute 1/3 cup water and
1/4 cup Chablis or other dry white wine for 1/2
cup water.

Almond Chicken

1 lb. skinless, boneless chicken
1 c. vegetable oil
5 slices fresh ginger root
3 green onions, chopped into 1-inch pieces
1 green pepper, chopped into 1-inch pieces
1/2 c. whole bamboo shoots, diced
1/3 c. Crisp Almonds (recipe follows)

Marinade

1/4 tsp. salt
1/8 tsp. pepper
1 tsp. cornstarch
1 tbsp. soy sauce
1 egg white

Seasoning sauce

1 tbsp. rice vinegar or white vinegar
2 tbsp. soy sauce
1 tbsp. rice wine or dry sherry
1/2 tsp. salt
1 tsp. sugar
1/2 tsp. cornstarch

Dice chicken into 1-inch cubes. Combine marinade ingredients in a medium bowl. Add chicken and mix well. Let stand 30 minutes.

Heat oil in a wok over high heat for 30 seconds. Add chicken to oil. Stir-fry until lightly browned. Remove chicken with a slotted spoon; drain well and set aside.

Remove all but 2 tablespoons oil from wok. Reheat oil over medium heat for 30 seconds. Add ginger, onions, pepper, and bamboo shoots to oil. Stir-fry 1–2 minutes until vegetables are tender–crisp.

Combine ingredients for seasoning sauce in a small bowl; mix well and add to wok. Bring to a boil. Add chicken to boiling sauce. Stir-fry until chicken is coated with sauce. Add almonds; mix well and serve hot. Makes 4 servings.

Crisp Almonds

4 c. oil for deep-frying
1 c. almond halves

Heat oil in a wok over medium heat to 350°F. Add nuts and stir 2–3 minutes until golden brown. Remove from hot oil and drain well on paper towels. Let stand 5 minutes before using.

Quick Chicken and Rice Dinner

4 boneless, skinless chicken breast halves
 (about 1 1/4 lb.)
1 tbsp. oil
1 can (10 3/4 oz.) condensed cream of chicken soup
1 1/3 c. water or milk
2 c. instant rice
2 c. frozen broccoli florets, thawed

Brown chicken in oil in large nonstick skillet on medium-high heat for 5 minutes on each side. Remove from skillet.

Add soup and water to skillet. Bring to a boil. Stir in rice and broccoli. Top with chicken; cover. Cook on low heat for 5 minutes. Stir and serve.

Zippy Orange Chicken and Rice

1/2 c. salad dressing, divided
4 boneless, skinless chicken breast halves
   (about 1 1/4 lb.), cut into strips
1/2 c. orange juice
2 tbsp. brown sugar
1 1/2 c. instant rice
1 green pepper, cut into strips
1 can (11 oz.) mandarin orange
   segments, drained
1 can (8 oz.) pineapple chunks, drained

Heat 2 tablespoons of dressing in skillet on medium-high heat. Add chicken; cook and stir 5 minutes or until no longer pink. Drain. Reduce heat to medium.

Mix remaining dressing, juice, and sugar. Stir into skillet. Add rice and green pepper; bring to boil. Remove from heat; add orange segments and pineapple. Let stand, covered, for 5 minutes. Makes 4 servings.

Lemon Basil Chicken

1 c. salad dressing
2 tbsp. fresh lemon juice
2 tsp. honey
1 tsp. dried basil leaves
1 broiler-fryer chicken (2 1/2 to 3 lb.), cut up

Heat oven to 375°F.

Mix salad dressing, juice, honey, and basil. Place chicken in 13x9-inch baking dish. Spread with salad dressing mixture. Bake 45 minutes or until chicken is cooked through.

Mushroom Chicken

4 boneless chicken breasts
1/4 c. chopped onions
2 cloves garlic
1 can condensed cream of mushroom soup
3/4 c. milk

In a deep frying pan (with lid) brown chicken breasts on medium to high heat until golden brown. Remove from pan.

Add onions and sauté for 3 minutes. Add garlic and cook for 1 minute more. Add soup to onion-garlic mixture and stir in milk. Heat until bubbly.

Add chicken to pan and submerge in sauce. Cover and cook for about 10 minutes or until chicken is cooked thoroughly. Serve over rice or noodles.

Dijon Chicken

1 whole chicken
3 tbsp. butter, melted
1 tsp. thyme
3 tbsp. red pepper sauce
3 tbsp. mustard
1 small onion, minced
1 1/2 c. bread crumbs

Slice chicken down back so that it lies flat. Brush chicken with butter and broil 5 minutes. Baste every 5 minutes until chicken has cooked 20 minutes (should be skin side down). Turn chicken over skin side up and baste. Add thyme and red pepper sauce. Cook skin side up for 10 minutes.

Preheat oven to 400°F. In a bowl, mix mustard, minced onion, and 2 tablespoons of juice from cooked chicken. Rub mixture on skin of chicken, then cover with bread crumbs. Bake about 20 minutes or until crumbs are brown.

Chicken and Garlic

1 lb. chicken parts, cut into serving pieces
1/2 c. white or cider vinegar
2 tbsp. soy sauce
5 cloves garlic, crushed
salt and pepper

Combine all ingredients in a saucepan. Bring to a boil and simmer until chicken is cooked and tender, about 20 minutes. Season with salt and pepper, if desired.

Serve with rice and a side of diced tomatoes and sliced scallions.

Baja California Chicken

4 tbsp. olive oil
4 tbsp. tarragon vinegar
2 cloves garlic
8 chicken breasts
seasoned salt and pepper
2/3 c. dry sherry

Preheat oven to 350°F.

Put oil and vinegar in a skillet and press garlic into the mixture.

While skillet is heating, sprinkle seasoned salt and pepper on chicken. Sauté chicken breasts until golden brown. Place chicken in a baking pan and pour sherry over chicken. Bake for 10 minutes.

Bistro Chicken with Feta

2 c. cooked penne or rotini pasta
1 c. quartered cherry tomatoes
1 pkg. (4 oz.) feta cheese, crumbled
1/2 c. prepared honey mustard or Caesar
   salad dressing
1/3 c. lightly packed fresh basil leaves,
   cut into strips
1/4 c. chopped red onion
1/4 c. sun-dried tomatoes, drained and chopped
2 boneless, skinless chicken breast halves,
   grilled or broiled, cut into 1/4-inch slices

Mix all ingredients. Serve warm or chilled.

Chicken Cordon Bleu

2 boneless chicken breasts
2 slices ham
2 slices Swiss cheese
fresh parsley, minced
1/8 tsp. garlic powder
salt
1/8 tsp. white pepper
2/3 tsp. vegetable oil
1/8 c. bread crumbs

Pound chicken breasts flat. Place one ham and one cheese slice on each chicken piece. Sprinkle with minced parsley, garlic powder, salt, and pepper. Roll up chicken to enclose ham and cheese. Secure with wooden toothpicks. Brush with oil. Bread with crumbs. Place on a nonstick baking sheet. Bake at 350°F for 35 minutes.

Chicken Diane

1/4 c. butter, divided
6 boneless, skinless chicken thighs or breast halves
1 medium onion, chopped fine
1/3 c. fresh parsley
1/4 c. steak sauce
1/4 c. dry sherry
1 tbsp. Worcestershire sauce
1 tbsp. Dijon mustard

In a large skillet, heat half the butter over medium heat until bubbly. Add chicken and cook, turning frequently, until lightly browned on all sides and juices run clear when pierced with a fork. Remove chicken to a plate and keep warm.

In same skillet, heat remaining butter. Add onion and sauté until translucent, about 2 minutes or less. Reduce heat and add all remaining ingredients except chicken. Cook, stirring occasionally, until heated through. Return chicken to skillet and turn to coat with sauce.

Serve with rice or noodles and a tossed salad.

Chicken Delfine

1 fryer, cut up
2 tbsp. olive oil
1 medium onion, sliced
1 clove garlic, minced
2 tbsp. tomato paste
1 can (12 oz.) tomato sauce
1/2 tsp. cinnamon
fresh oregano
salt and pepper to taste

Brown chicken in olive oil and remove from pan. Add onion and garlic; sauté until translucent. Add tomato paste and mix well. Add tomato sauce, cinnamon, and oregano. Mix well and add chicken with juices.

Cover and reduce heat. Simmer until chicken is done (about 30–40 minutes).

Chicken Stir-Fry

3/4 c. peanut oil
2 lb. boneless, skinless chicken breasts
1/8 tsp. garlic powder
1/8 tsp. onion powder
1/8 tsp. black pepper
2 tbsp. sugar
1 c. chicken broth
1 medium onion, chopped
12 green onions, chopped
1/3 c. soy sauce

Put peanut oil in wok, and put on stove on highest heat. (Keep the heat on high through the entire cooking time.) When oil is hot, add chicken and cook until tender and no longer pink. While cooking, sprinkle garlic powder, onion powder, and black pepper on chicken. Add sugar while cooking. When the chicken is brown, add chicken broth and vegetables. Cook for 3–4 minutes more or until broth begins to steam. Add soy sauce. Serve hot over rice.

Note: If you prefer a thicker sauce, use a mixture of cornstarch and water to thicken just before removing from heat.

Mediterranean Chicken Breasts

1/2 c. (2 oz.) grated Romano cheese
1/4 c. dry bread crumbs
1 tsp. dried basil leaves
1/4 tsp. paprika
1/4 tsp. salt
1/4 tsp. ground black pepper
3 tbsp. olive oil
6 boneless, skinless chicken breast halves
  (about 2 lb.)

Mix cheese, crumbs, and seasonings. Dip chicken in oil; coat with cheese mixture.

Spray skillet with cooking spray. Add chicken and cook on medium heat, 5–7 minutes on each side or until cooked through.

Makes 6 servings.

Italian Chicken Breasts

1/2 c. (2 oz.) grated Parmesan cheese
1/4 c. dry bread crumbs
1 tsp. dried oregano leaves
1 tsp. parsley flakes
1/4 tsp. paprika
1/4 tsp. salt
1/4 tsp. ground black pepper
2 tbsp. butter, melted
6 boneless, skinless chicken breast halves
  (about 2 lb.)

Heat oven to 400°F. Spray a 15x10x1-inch baking pan with cooking spray.

Mix cheese, crumbs, and seasonings. Dip chicken in butter; coat with crumb mixture. Place in prepared pan. Bake 20–25 minutes, or until cooked through.

Quick Chicken Marinara

1 tbsp. olive oil
2 boneless, skinless chicken breast halves (about 3/4 lb.), cut into strips
1 yellow or green pepper, cut into strips
1 jar (15 oz.) marinara sauce
1 pkg. (9 oz.) spinach fettucini, cooked and drained

Heat oil in skillet on medium-high heat. Add chicken and pepper; cook and stir 3 minutes.

Stir in sauce. Cook on medium heat 3–5 minutes or until chicken is cooked through. Serve over hot fettucini. Top with Parmesan cheese, if desired.

Makes 4 servings.

Oven-Fried Cornflake Chicken

3 lb. fryer chicken, cut up
2 large eggs, slightly beaten
4 tbsp. milk
2 1/2 c. cornflakes, crushed
2 tsp. salt
1/2 tsp. pepper
5 tbsp. butter, melted

Preheat oven to 350°F. Wash chicken and pat dry. Mix eggs and milk. In a separate bowl combine cornflake crumbs, salt, and pepper.

Dip chicken into milk and egg mixture then into crumb mixture, coating each piece evenly. Set in well-greased baking pan.

Drizzle with melted butter. Bake, uncovered, for 1 hour.

Perfect Tuna Casserole

1 can cream of mushroom soup
1/3 c. milk
6 1/2 oz. tuna, drained and flaked
2 eggs, hard-boiled and sliced
1 c. peas, cooked
1 c. potato chips, slightly crumbled

Preheat oven to 350°F. Blend soup and milk in
1-quart casserole. Stir in tuna, eggs, and peas. Bake
20 minutes. Top with chips; bake 10 minutes longer.

Avery Island Deviled Shrimp

1/4 c. butter plus 2 tbsp.
1 lb. breaded shrimp
1 medium onion, chopped fine
1 clove garlic, minced
1 can (10 1/2 oz.) beef consommé
1/2 c. water
2 tbsp. Worcestershire sauce
1 1/2 tsp. prepared mustard
1/2 tsp. salt
1/2 tsp. hot red pepper sauce
juice of one small lemon
3 c. long-grain white rice, cooked and hot

Melt 1/4 cup butter in skillet over low heat; add
shrimp and cook until browned. Remove from heat
and keep warm.

Melt 2 tablespoons butter in a saucepan over low
heat; add onion and garlic. Sauté over medium heat
until tender. Add all remaining ingredients except
lemon juice and rice. Heat to boiling; reduce heat
and simmer for 15 minutes or until liquid is reduced
to about 1 cup. Add lemon juice. Place rice on a
serving platter. Top rice with shrimp, then sauce.

Easy Crab Dish

2 pkg. frozen chopped spinach, thawed
1 c. onion, chopped fine
1 lb. crabmeat
1 1/2 c. sharp cheddar cheese, grated
dash nutmeg
salt and freshly ground pepper to taste
1 carton sour cream
fresh dill, chopped

In a casserole dish, layer half of spinach,
half of onion, half of crab, and half of cheese.
Season with nutmeg, salt, and pepper.

Add remaining spinach, onion, crab, and
cheese in same order. Bake at 350°F for about
35 minutes. Top with sour cream and fresh dill,
if desired.

Salmon Patties

1 lb. canned pink or red salmon
pinch salt
1 small onion, diced
1/4 c. bread crumbs, plain or spiced
2 eggs
1 tsp. lemon juice

Combine all ingredients in a bowl. Form approximately 8 patties, each about 1/2 to 3/4-inch
thick and 2 1/2 to 3 inches in diameter. Fry in oil
or butter until brown and crispy.

Oven method: Place patties in a well-greased
pan. Bake at 400°F for about 15 minutes or until
brown.

Buffalo Chicken Wings

24 chicken wings
4 c. oil
4 tbsp. butter
2–5 tbsp. hot sauce
1 tbsp. white vinegar
2 1/2 c. Blue Cheese Dressing (recipe follows)
celery sticks

Discard small tip of each wing; split at large joint, and sprinkle with salt and pepper.

Heat oil in large casserole or fryer. Add half of wings and cook, stirring occasionally. When brown and crisp (15–20 minutes), remove and drain well. Cook remaining wings.

Melt butter in saucepan; add hot sauce and vinegar.

Put wings on a warm platter and pour sauce over them (or put wings and sauce in a closed container and shake).

Serve with celery sticks and Blue Cheese Dressing (for dipping).

Lower Fat Variation:

Broil or grill wings instead of frying.

Mix 1/2 cup hot sauce, 4 tablespoons honey, 2 tablespoons vinegar, 2 tablespoons lemon juice, and 1 heaping teaspoon dry mustard.

Heat sauce until it thickens, then add wings, cooking for 10 minutes.

Blue Cheese Dressing

1 c. Homemade Mayonnaise (recipe follows)
2 tbsp. finely chopped onion
1 tsp. finely minced garlic
1/4 c. finely chopped parsley
1/2 c. sour cream
1 tbsp. lemon juice
1 tbsp. white vinegar
1/4 c. crumbled blue cheese
salt, pepper and cayenne to taste

Combine and chill for 1 hour or longer.

Makes 2 1/2 cups.

Homemade Mayonnaise

1 egg yolk
1 tsp. Dijon mustard
salt and freshly ground pepper
1 tsp. vinegar or lemon juice
1 c. oil

Beat egg yolk, mustard, salt, pepper, and vinegar or lemon juice for a few seconds with a wire whisk or beater.

Add oil gradually and continue beating to correct consistency.

Makes 1 cup.

Simple Buffalo Wings

3 lb. frozen, disjointed chicken wings
8–10 oz. hot sauce

Bring deep fryer to 450°F and place 1 pound of frozen wings into fryer (add more or less depending on size of fryer). Cook 8–10 minutes. Remember, the hotter the grease is, the faster the chicken wings will cook and the less grease they will absorb.

Put 3–4 ounces of hot sauce in a heavy, plastic bowl (must have a sealable lid). Remove the fully cooked wings from the deep fryer. Place the wings in the bowl and seal the lid. Be sure to hold the lid on tightly. Shake until wings are fully coated. Serve with blue cheese dressing.

Chicken Quesadillas

8 tortillas
2 tbsp. oil
1 1/2 c. chopped cooked chicken
1 1/2 c. shredded Monterey Jack or
   mozzarella cheese
1/2 c. medium salsa

Brush one side of each of 4 tortillas with oil. Place on a baking sheet, oiled side down. Spread chicken over the tortillas and sprinkle with cheese. Divide salsa over the cheese. Top with remaining tortillas and press down to form a tortilla sandwich. Brush tops with oil. Bake in a 500°F oven for about 5 minutes, or until the tortillas are golden brown. Cut into wedges.

Makes 4 servings.

Mexican Chicken and Rice

4 boneless, skinless chicken breast halves
   (about 1 1/4 lb.)
1 c. salsa
1 c. chicken broth
2 c. instant rice
1 c. (4 oz.) shredded cheddar cheese

Bring chicken, salsa, and broth to a boil in large skillet; cover. Simmer 10 minutes. Return to a boil. Stir in rice. Sprinkle with cheese; cover. Cook on low heat for 5 minutes.

Chicken Tacos

4 boneless, skinless chicken breast halves
   (about 1 1/4 lb.), cut into 1/2-inch pieces
1 pkg. (1 1/4 oz.) taco seasoning mix
3/4 c. water
12 taco shells
1 pkg. (8 oz.) Mexican-style shredded cheese
shredded lettuce and chopped tomatoes

Spray a 10-inch skillet with cooking spray. Add chicken; cook on medium heat until cooked through. Stir in seasoning mix and water. Cook 10 minutes, stirring occasionally, until sauce is slightly thickened.

Spoon 2 tablespoons chicken mixture into each taco shell. Sprinkle with cheese. Top with shredded lettuce and chopped tomatoes.

Chicken Flautas

2 c. cooked chicken, shredded
2/3 c. salsa
1/4 c. green onion, sliced
3/4 tsp. ground cumin
vegetable oil for frying
32 corn tortillas
2 c. cheddar or Monterey Jack cheese, shredded
guacamole

Combine chicken, salsa, onion, and cumin; mix well. Heat about 1/2 inch of oil in small skillet until hot but not smoking. Quickly fry each tortilla in oil to soften, about 2 seconds on each side. Drain on paper towels. Spoon 1 tablespoon chicken mixture and 1 tablespoon cheese down center of each tortilla. Roll tightly; secure with wooden pick. Place seam-side down on baking sheet. Bake in preheated oven at 400°F for 18–20 minutes or until crisp. Serve warm with guacamole and additional salsa.

Mexican Chicken Pizza

2 boneless, skinless chicken breasts, cubed
1 1/2 c. salsa
1 (12-inch) pizza crust
1/2 c. red pepper strips
1 tsp. chopped cilantro
1 pkg. (4 oz.) shredded mozzarella cheese
1 pkg. (4 oz.) shredded cheddar cheese

Spray large skillet with cooking spray. Add chicken; cook on medium heat until chicken is cooked through. Stir in salsa; cook on low heat for 5 minutes. Spoon chicken mixture over pizza crust; sprinkle with red pepper and cilantro. Top with cheeses. Bake at 400°F for 10–15 minutes, or until cheese is melted.

Citrus Salmon

1 lb. salmon fillets
salt and pepper
1 tbsp. cornstarch
1 tbsp. water
2 tbsp. frozen orange juice concentrate, undiluted
1 tbsp. lemon juice
1/4 c. brown sugar

Sprinkle both sides of salmon fillets with salt and pepper. Mix cornstarch and water in a small bowl to form a paste. Add orange juice concentrate, lemon juice, and brown sugar. Stir mixture well until all ingredients are dissolved. Set aside.

Pour half of sauce into bottom of a microwave-safe dish. Place salmon fillets in the dish on top of sauce. Pour remaining sauce over salmon. Cover dish with plastic wrap. Vent to allow steam to escape. Microwave on high for 7–10 minutes. Remove from microwave and remove plastic wrap. Place fillets on a plate. Stir remaining sauce and pour over the fillets. Garnish with parsley or orange slices if desired.

Chicken Tortilla Bake

1 can (10 3/4 oz.) tomato soup
1 c. salsa
1/2 c. milk
1 lb. skinless, boneless chicken breasts, cut into cubes
8 (6-inch) corn tortillas, cut into quarters
1 c. (4 oz.) cheddar cheese, shredded and divided

In a 2-quart shallow baking dish, mix soup, salsa, milk, chicken, tortillas, and half of cheese. Cover and bake at 400°F for 30 minutes, or until chicken is no longer pink. Top with remaining cheese.

Avocado–Salmon Sandwich

1 ripe avocado
juice of 1 lemon, divided
6 hamburger buns, split
2 cans (7 3/4 oz. ea.) sockeye salmon
6 slices Swiss cheese
sesame seeds

Preheat broiler to 475°F. Peel and slice avocado; sprinkle with part of lemon juice. Divide avocado slices evenly over bottoms of hamburger buns.

Drain salmon and break into chunks. Divide evenly over avocado slices and sprinkle with remaining lemon juice. Top with second halves of buns, then with cheese slices. Sprinkle with sesame seeds. Broil about 8 inches from heat until cheese melts and sandwiches are heated through. Garnish with dill pickles.

Shrimp and Okra Creole

1 pkg. (14 oz.) macaroni and cheese dinner
1/2 c. chopped green pepper
1/2 c. chopped okra, fresh or frozen
1 can (14 1/2 oz.) tomatoes, crushed
1 lb. small shrimp, cooked
1/2 tsp. hot pepper sauce

Prepare macaroni and cheese dinner as directed on package. Set aside.

Coat a nonstick skillet with cooking spray. Add green pepper and okra, cooking and stirring until slightly crisp.

Stir vegetables and remaining ingredients into prepared macaroni and cheese. Cook on medium heat until thoroughly heated.

Shrimp Scampi

1/4 c. lemon juice
1/4 c. water
1/4 c. olive oil, divided
1 envelope garlic and herb salad dressing mix
2 tbsp. chopped fresh parsley
1 tsp. minced garlic (optional)
1/8 tsp. black pepper
1 small onion, chopped
1 lb. shrimp, cleaned

Mix lemon juice, water, 2 tablespoons of olive oil, salad dressing mix, parsley, garlic, and pepper in medium bowl. Stir until well blended; set aside.

Heat remaining 2 tablespoons of oil in a large skillet on medium heat. Add onion; cook and stir until tender but not browned. Add shrimp; cook 3 minutes or until shrimp turn pink, stirring occasionally. Stir in dressing mixture.

Bring to boil over medium heat; boil 1 minute. Serve over rice or pasta.

Crab and Avocado Melts

3 c. shredded cheddar cheese, divided
1 can (6 oz.) crabmeat, rinsed, drained, and flaked
1/3 c. green bell pepper, chopped fine
6 slices bacon, cooked and crumbled
2/3 c. sour cream
1/2 c. mayonnaise
salt and pepper to taste
2 avocados, seeded, peeled, and sliced
5 English muffins, split and lightly toasted

Combine 1 cup cheese, crab meat, green pepper, bacon, sour cream, mayonnaise, and salt and pepper in a large bowl. Spoon crab mixture over muffin halves. Top each with avocado slices and remaining cheese. Broil 3–5 minutes, or just until cheese melts.

Pasta

Butterfly:
To cut almost but not completely through the center
of a piece of meat, so that when the two halves
are spread they resemble a butterfly.

Chill:
To reduce the temperature by refrigerating or placing over ice.

Easy Chicken and Pasta

1 tbsp. vegetable oil
1 lb. skinless, boneless chicken breasts, cut up
1 can (10 3/4 oz.) cream of chicken soup
1/2 c. water
1 bag (16 oz.) frozen seasoned pasta
  and vegetable combination

Heat oil in medium skillet over medium-high heat. Add chicken and cook until browned, stirring often. Remove chicken and set aside.

Add soup, water, and pasta-vegetable combination to skillet. Heat to a boil. Return chicken to skillet. Reduce heat to low. Cover and cook 5 minutes or until chicken is no longer pink, stirring occasionally.

Buffalo Chicken Pasta

1 lb. mostaccioli
1 tsp. paprika
1/2 tsp. salt
1/2 tsp. garlic powder
1/2 tsp. black pepper
1 lb. boneless, skinless chicken breasts,
  cut into 1/2-inch pieces
2 tsp. vegetable oil, divided
1–2 tsp. hot sauce
1 c. sliced celery
1/2 c. chopped red onion
1 c. mayonnaise
1/2 c. blue cheese salad dressing
3/4 c. milk
2 tbsp. blue cheese, crumbled

Prepare pasta according to package directions. While pasta is cooking, combine paprika, salt, garlic powder, and pepper; sprinkle over chicken, stirring to coat. Add 1 teaspoon oil to a large skillet and heat over medium-high heat. Add chicken to skillet and sauté over medium-high heat, stirring frequently, until chicken is golden brown and cooked through, about 4 minutes. Add hot sauce and cook 1 minute more. Remove chicken from skillet. Add remaining oil to skillet. Add celery and onion; sauté for 2 minutes.

Combine mayonnaise, salad dressing, and milk in a small bowl. Add to vegetables in skillet. Add chicken. Stir constantly and cook over medium-low heat until thoroughly heated. When pasta is done, drain and return to pot. Add contents of skillet to pot and mix well. Transfer to serving dish and sprinkle with cheese. Serve immediately.

Chicken Cacciatore Macaroni

1 pkg. (7 1/4 oz.) macaroni and cheese dinner
1/4 c. margarine
1/4 c. milk
1 c. chopped, cooked chicken
1 c. canned seasoned tomatoes, chopped
1/3 c. chopped green pepper

Prepare macaroni and cheese dinner as directed on package using margarine and milk. Stir in remaining ingredients.

Makes 4 servings.

Ziti with Chicken

1 lb. ziti
2 tsp. butter
1 medium onion, chopped
1 tbsp. Dijon mustard
2 tbsp. all-purpose flour
2 c. low-sodium chicken broth
1/4 c. lemon juice
1 pkg (10 oz.) frozen peas, defrosted
  and drained
1/4 c. fresh parsley, chopped
12 oz. chopped, cooked chicken
salt and pepper to taste

Prepare pasta according to package directions. While pasta is cooking, warm butter over medium heat in a large skillet. Add onion and cook for 3 minutes. Stir in Dijon mustard and flour. Very gradually whisk in chicken broth. Bring broth to a boil and stir in lemon juice, peas, and parsley. When pasta is done, drain it well. Toss pasta and cooked chicken with sauce; season with salt and pepper. Serve.

Chicken Spaghetti

1 pkg. (12 oz.) spaghetti
3 cans (5 oz. ea.) chicken
3 tbsp. flour
3 tbsp. butter
1/4 c. milk
1 can cream of chicken soup
1 can cream of mushroom soup
8 oz. shredded cheddar cheese, divided
8 oz. shredded mozzarella cheese, divided

Cook spaghetti according to package directions. While spaghetti is cooking, mix chicken, flour, butter, milk, and soups in a large 4 to 6-quart pan over medium heat to melt butter. Then add 4 ounces each of cheddar and mozzarella. Mix well.

After spaghetti is cooked, add it to chicken mixture. Pour into a 13x9-inch pan. Top with remaining cheeses. Bake at 350°F for 20–25 minutes or until cheese is melted.

Cheesy Pasta and Broccoli

1/2 lb. spaghetti, broken in half
1 pkg. (16 oz.) frozen broccoli florets
1 c. (8 oz.) cheese sauce

Cook spaghetti according to package directions, adding broccoli during last 6 minutes of cooking time. Drain. Heat cheese sauce in microwave as directed on label. Pour over spaghetti and broccoli. Toss until thoroughly coated.

Spaghetti and Turkey Almondine

8 oz. spaghetti
2 tsp. margarine
1/2 c. sliced almonds, toasted
1 tbsp. vegetable oil
8 oz. smoked turkey, cut into strips
8 oz. fresh-cut green beans, steamed just
  until tender
1/2 medium red onion, sliced thin
1/2 tsp. dried tarragon leaves
1/4 c. Italian salad dressing

Cook pasta according to package directions; drain. In medium nonstick skillet, melt margarine. Add almonds; toss to coat. Cook over medium heat just until golden. Remove and set aside. In same skillet, heat oil. Add next four ingredients; stir-fry over medium-high heat until vegetables are tender. Stir in almonds and tarragon. Add pasta and salad dressing; stir well to mix. Heat through. Arrange on warm serving platter and serve immediately.

Mustard Butter Pasta

1 pkg. fettucini
3/4 c. chopped vegetables
2 tbsp. butter, softened
4 tbsp. Dijon mustard

Boil pasta and any boilable vegetables in same water. Sauté any other vegetables briefly.

While pasta is boiling, mix mustard and butter thoroughly. Blend well into the drained pasta and vegetables.

Parmesan Pasta

8 oz. spaghetti
1 clove garlic, minced
1/4 c. (1/2 stick) butter
3/4 c. (3 oz.) grated Parmesan cheese
fresh parsley
diced tomatoes
additional cheese (optional)

Prepare spaghetti as directed on package. Drain.

In a pan over medium heat, cook and stir garlic in butter until tender. Add spaghetti and toss lightly. Sprinkle with cheese; toss to coat. Sprinkle with chopped fresh parsley, diced tomatoes, and additional cheese, if desired. Serve immediately.

Makes 4 servings.

Fresh Tomato Sauce with Mint and Garlic on Spaghetti

4 garlic cloves, minced
3 tbsp. extra virgin olive oil, divided
3 lb. tomatoes, peeled, seeded, and chopped
1/2 tsp. salt
1/2 tsp. freshly ground pepper
1 tbsp. fresh mint leaves, chopped
3/4 lb. spaghetti

In a large skillet, place garlic and 2 tablespoons of oil. Cook over low heat until garlic is fragrant, about 2 minutes. Increase heat to high and cook until garlic is golden, about 10 seconds longer. Add tomatoes and cook over high heat, stirring occasionally, until sauce is thick but chunky and some tomato liquid still remains, about 10 minutes. Turn off heat and season with the pepper and mint.

In a large saucepan of boiling salted water, cook spaghetti until tender but still firm, about 8 minutes. Drain and toss with remaining olive oil. Reheat sauce over moderate heat. Place pasta in a large serving bowl and toss with a third of sauce. Pour remaining sauce over spaghetti; toss lightly and serve.

Alfredo with Roasted Red Peppers

1 pkg. (10 oz.) alfredo sauce
1 jar (7 oz.) roasted red peppers, drained and sliced
1/3 c. plus 2 tbsp. toasted, chopped walnuts
1 pkg. (9 oz.) prepared cheese ravioli,
  cooked and drained
fresh parsley, chopped

Heat sauce, peppers, and 1/3 cup of walnuts. Toss with ravioli. Sprinkle with 2 tablespoons walnuts and fresh parsley.

Roasted Red Pepper Sauce for Pasta

1 jar (7 oz.) roasted red peppers, drained
1 c. ricotta cheese
1 small clove garlic
1 tbsp. olive oil
1/4 tsp. salt
1/4 tsp. ground white pepper
1 tbsp. fresh basil, chopped fine

Place all ingredients except basil in blender or food processor; cover. Blend until puréed. Stir in basil. Pour into saucepan; heat thoroughly on low heat. Toss with hot cooked pasta.

Makes 2 cups sauce (enough for 12 ounces of cooked pasta).

Broccoli Pepper Macaroni

1 pkg. (7 1/4 oz.) macaroni and cheese dinner
1 c. frozen chopped broccoli, cooked and drained
1/4 c. chopped red pepper
1/4 c. chopped green pepper
1/8 tsp. dill weed (optional)

Prepare macaroni and cheese dinner as directed on package. Stir in remaining ingredients.

Makes 4 servings.

Pasta with Mushrooms and Green Beans

1/2 c. red wine
1 1/2 lb. fresh green beans, cleaned and cut into 1 1/2-inch pieces
1/2 lb. fresh mushrooms, cleaned and sliced
1 onion, sliced
5 cloves garlic, minced
2 tsp. dried basil
1 tsp. dried marjoram

freshly ground black pepper
1 can (32 oz.) crushed tomatoes
1 lb. pasta

Put wine in a large skillet or Dutch oven. Add next 7 ingredients. Let simmer, covered, for 10–15 minutes. Add crushed tomatoes. Let simmer 30 minutes. Cook pasta in unsalted, unoiled water. Combine and enjoy.

Pasta Primavera

1 bottle (8 oz.) Italian dressing
3/4 c. salad dressing
1 tsp. Italian seasoning
4 c. broccoli florets
4 c. (8 oz.) bow tie pasta, cooked and drained
1 c. carrot slices
1 c. chopped red pepper
4 oz. provolone cheese, cubed
1/2 c. sliced red onion

Mix dressings and seasoning until well blended. Add remaining ingredients; mix lightly. Refrigerate until ready to serve.

Easy Chicken Fettucini

8 oz. plain or spinach fettucini
2 skinless, boneless chicken breast halves (about 3/4 lb.), cut into chunks
1/2 c. milk
1/4 c. butter, softened
3/4 c. (3 oz.) grated Parmesan cheese
3/4 tsp. garlic powder
1/4 tsp. pepper

Cook fettucini as directed on package; drain. While pasta is cooking, cook chicken in skillet sprayed with cooking spray until cooked through.
Add milk and butter to hot fettucini. Stir in chicken, Parmesan, and seasonings.
Makes 6 servings.

Bacon and Creamy Fettucini

1 pkg. (16 oz.) bacon, cut into 1/2-inch pieces
8 oz. mushrooms, sliced
6 green onions, sliced
8 oz. fettucini, uncooked
1 pkg. (8 oz.) cream cheese, cubed
2/3 c. skim milk
1/2 tsp. garlic powder
1/2 tsp. dried basil
1/2 tsp. thyme leaves
1 small tomato, chopped

Cook bacon until crisp. Drain. Add mushrooms and onions. Cook and stir 4 minutes. Set aside.

Cook fettucini as directed on package in large saucepan or Dutch oven. Drain. Return noodles to saucepan and add all remaining ingredients except bacon mixture and tomato. Cook and stir over medium heat until cheese melts. Toss bacon mixture with fettucini; sprinkle with tomato. Makes 8 servings.

Parmesan Fettucini Alfredo

8 oz. fettucini
3/4 c. grated Parmesan cheese
1/3 c. half-and-half
3 tbsp. butter, melted
dash ground nutmeg
dash pepper

Prepare fettucini as directed on package. Drain and return to pan.

Add cheese, half-and-half, and butter; toss to coat. Sprinkle with nutmeg and pepper. Serve immediately with additional Parmesan cheese, if desired. Makes 4 servings.

Fettucini Alfredo

1 c. heavy cream
2 tbsp. sweet butter
3/4 c. freshly grated Parmesan cheese, divided
freshly ground black pepper
fettucini

Bring cream and butter to a boil in a sauté pan. Reduce heat and simmer for 30 seconds. Add half of Parmesan and a little pepper; whisk until smooth, then remove from heat. Set aside.

Cook fettucini according to package directions. Drain and add pasta to cream mixture. Add remaining Parmesan. Toss well and serve immediately.

Note: Do not substitute canned grated Parmesan cheese for freshly grated cheese. Canned Parmesan will not melt.

Fettucini with Zucchini and Mushrooms

1 lb. pkg. fettucini
1/2 c. butter
1/2 lb. mushrooms
1 1/4 lb. zucchini
1 c. half-and-half
3/4 c. Parmesan cheese
1/2 c. parsley

Cook fettucini *al dente*. While pasta is cooking, cut zucchini into julienne strips. Sauté mushrooms and zucchini in butter for 2 minutes. Add half-and-half to sauté; reduce heat and simmer for 3 minutes. Add cooked fettucini, cheese, and parsley. Toss to mix well.

Spicy Shrimp Alfredo

1/4 lb. small shrimp
1/2 stick butter
1/4 tsp. garlic powder
1 tbsp. hot sauce
1/2 tsp. black pepper
1/3 c. Parmesan cheese
1/2 c. whipping cream
1 pkg. fettucini

Cook shrimp in a saucepan for 5 minutes with butter, garlic powder, hot sauce, and black pepper. Remove shrimp and set aside.

Add Parmesan and whipping cream to sauce in pan. Simmer until thick. Cook fettucini as directed on package. Toss well with sauce and shrimp.

Angel Hair Pasta with Scallops

4 slices bacon, diced fine
3 cloves garlic, minced
1/2 lb. sea scallops, sliced 1/4-inch thick
1 medium or 2 small fresh tomatoes, diced
    into 1/4-inch pieces
fresh thyme, salt, and pepper to taste
1 lb. angel hair pasta
extra–virgin olive oil
Parmesan cheese, freshly grated

Boil water for pasta. When it begins to boil, add salt and oil, then turn down heat and start sauce. In a large skillet over medium heat, cook bacon and render out some of the grease. Add garlic and stir to brown. Add scallops, cooking thoroughly but quickly to avoid browning.

When scallops are almost done, turn water back up to a boil. Add tomatoes to scallops; at the same time, put the pasta into water. Cook pasta according to the package directions (about 2–3 minutes for fresh pasta, 6–7 minutes for dried). Drain pasta and *lightly* oil it with extra–virgin olive oil (to keep pasta from clumping). Toss fresh thyme into skillet and stir through before removing it from heat.

Toss pasta with sauce, and serve with freshly grated Parmesan cheese.

Asparagus and Shrimp with Penne Pasta

1 envelope garlic and herb salad dressing mix
6 asparagus spears, cut into 1-inch pieces
1/2 lb. medium shrimp, cleaned
1 small red pepper, cut into thin strips
8 oz. penne or ziti pasta
1 pkg. (4 oz.) feta cheese, crumbled

Prepare salad dressing mix as directed on envelope.

Heat 1 tablespoon of prepared dressing in large nonstick skillet over medium heat. Add asparagus; cook and stir for 3 minutes. Add shrimp and red pepper; cover. Cook 5 minutes or until shrimp are pink and vegetables are tender-crisp, stirring occasionally.

Meanwhile, cook pasta as directed on package; drain. Place in large serving bowl. Toss with remaining dressing, shrimp mixture, and cheese. Serve immediately, or refrigerate and serve chilled.

Makes 4–6 servings.

Shrimp Creole Macaroni

1 pkg. (14 oz.) macaroni and cheese dinner
1/2 c. skim milk
1/2 c. chopped green pepper
1/4 c. chopped onion
1 tbsp. soft butter
1 can (14 1/2 oz.) stewed tomatoes,
 drained and chopped
1/2 lb. medium shrimp, cooked
1/2 tsp. hot pepper sauce

Prepare macaroni and cheese as directed on
package, omitting butter and milk and using
1/2 cup skim milk instead. Set aside and keep
warm. In a small frying pan, sauté green pepper
and onion in butter until tender-crisp. Add,
along with remaining ingredients, to macaroni.
Stir over medium heat until thoroughly heated.

Pesto Romano

2 c. fresh basil leaves
2 cloves garlic
1/4 c. pine nuts
1/4 tsp. salt
1/4 tsp. ground black pepper
1/2 c. olive oil
1 c. (4 oz.) grated Romano cheese
1 lb. radiatore (radiator-shaped pasta)

Place basil, garlic, pine nuts, salt, and pepper
in food processor fitted with steel blade; cover.
Process just until smooth. Drizzle olive oil in
slowly while food processor is running.
Transfer to mixing bowl; stir in cheese.
Cook pasta as directed on package; drain.
Toss hot pasta with pesto until well coated.
Makes 6 servings.

Lasagne

8 c. milk
1 clove garlic, cut in half
3/4 c. unsalted butter
1 c. flour
1 1/4 tsp. salt
1/4 tsp. white pepper
1/8 tsp. nutmeg
2 c. grated Parmesan cheese, divided
1/4 c. parsley, minced
2 pkg. (10 oz. ea.) frozen mixed vegetables,
 thawed and drained
2 pkg. (10 oz. ea.) frozen chopped broccoli,
 thawed and drained
24 oz. lasagne, cooked, rinsed, and drained
2 tbsp. unsalted butter

Heat milk and garlic in saucepan over medium heat
until milk just begins to bubble. Remove from heat;
discard garlic.

In another large saucepan, melt butter over medium
heat. Stir in flour, salt, pepper, and nutmeg. Cook for
2-3 minutes or until bubbly, stirring constantly. Add
hot garlic-milk mixture, stirring until smooth; reduce
heat. Simmer for 10 minutes or until thickened,
stirring constantly. Stir in 1 1/3 cups Parmesan
cheese and parsley.

Spread 1/3 cup sauce into each of two 3-quart
baking pans. Add mixed vegetables and broccoli to
remaining sauce, stirring to coat. Alternate layers of
noodles and vegetable-sauce mixture in each pan
until all ingredients are used. Dot top of each pan
with 1 tablespoon butter and sprinkle evenly with
remaining Parmesan cheese. Bake at 350°F
for 30-45 minutes or until bubbly.

Baked Spaghetti

1 c. onion, chopped
1 c. green pepper, chopped
1 tbsp. butter
1 can (28 oz.) tomatoes with liquid, cut up
1 can (4 oz.) mushrooms, drained
1 can (2 1/4 oz.) sliced ripe olives, drained
2 tsp. dried oregano
1 lb. ground beef, browned and drained
12 oz. spaghetti, cooked and drained
2 c. (8 oz.) cheddar cheese, shredded
1 can (10 3/4 oz.) condensed cream of
  mushroom soup
1/4 c. water
1/4 cup grated Parmesan cheese

In a large skillet, sauté onion and green
pepper in butter until tender. Add tomatoes,
mushrooms, olives, and oregano. Add browned
ground beef. Simmer, uncovered, for
10 minutes.

Place half of cooked spaghetti into a greased,
13x9x2-inch casserole. Top with half of vegetable mixture. Sprinkle with 1 cup of cheddar
cheese. Repeat layers.

Mix soup and water until smooth; pour over
casserole. Sprinkle with Parmesan cheese.
Bake, uncovered, at 350° F for 30-35 minutes
or until heated through.

Ham and Sour Cream Baked Noodles

1/2 lb. noodles, cooked and drained
1 1/2 c. cottage cheese
1 1/2 c. sour cream
2 c. ham, chopped
2 eggs, slightly beaten
1/2 tsp. salt

1/2 c. green bell pepper, chopped
1/2 c. celery, chopped fine
1/4 c. onion, chopped fine
pepper to taste
6 tbsp. butter, melted

Preheat oven to 350° F. Grease a 3-quart casserole.

Put cooked noodles into a bowl and toss with
remaining ingredients until well mixed. Spoon into
casserole and bake 50-60 minutes or until bubbling
and set.

Baked Ziti

1 lb. ground turkey
1 lb. Italian sausage
1 large onion, diced
1 medium green pepper, chopped
1 jar (29 oz.) spaghetti sauce
1 tsp. dried sweet basil leaf
1 tsp. dried oregano
3/4 tsp. garlic powder
1 lb. ziti
1 lb. mozzarella cheese, shredded
Parmesan cheese to taste

Break up and brown meats and vegetables together
until just brown. Add spaghetti sauce and simmer.
Add spices to taste.

Prepare pasta according to package directions.
Combine cooked pasta with meat and mozzarrella
in a large, greased baking dish. Bake at 350°F for
30-45 minutes. Serve with Parmesan cheese to taste.

Sesame Noodles

1 tsp. sesame oil
3-4 cloves fresh garlic, minced
1 c. sesame paste (or Tahini)
1/4 c. soy sauce
3 c. precooked oriental noodles
1 c. tea, freshly brewed
cucumber and bell pepper slivers (optional)

Heat oil in a saucepan. Fry garlic in oil until lightly browned. Add sesame paste and soy sauce. Cook until oil just starts to come out of paste. Pour over noodles and toss. If mixture is too thick, add tea. Chill and serve. Garnish with cucumber and bell pepper, if desired.

Spaghetti Casserole

2 lb. spaghetti, cooked and drained
1/2 lb. saltine crackers, coarsely crushed
grated Parmesan cheese
1 lb. sharp cheese
1 1/3 c. milk
butter

Preheat oven to 350° F. Spread half of spaghetti in a casserole dish. Cover with half of cracker crumbs. Sprinkle liberally with Parmesan cheese. Break 1 slice of sharp cheese into small pieces and lay on top. Pour half of milk over top. Layer remaining spaghetti, cracker crumbs, and Parmesan cheese. Top with remaining milk. Top casserole with sharp cheese by inserting each piece slightly down side, then allowing it to cover top.

Cover completely, using as much cheese as desired. Bake until cheese is golden brown. Let stand for 5 minutes before slicing. Top each slice with butter before serving.

Cheesy Sausage and Tortellini Toss

1 c. dried tri-color or plain tortellini
    (about 1/2 of a 7-oz. pkg.)
3 c. broccoli florets
8 oz. smoked Polish sausage, fully cooked,
    halved lengthwise and sliced thin on the bias
1 tbsp. butter
1 tbsp. all-purpose flour
1 tsp. caraway seed
1 c. milk
1 c. (4 oz.) process Swiss cheese, shredded
1 tbsp. coarse-grain brown mustard

In a Dutch oven or large saucepan, cook tortellini in boiling salted water for 10 minutes, stirring occasionally. Add broccoli and Polish sausage. Return to boiling and cook, stirring occasionally, about 5 minutes more or until pasta is tender but slightly firm and broccoli is tender-crisp. Drain and keep warm. Melt butter in a medium saucepan. Stir in flour and caraway seed. Add milk all at once. Cook and stir until thickened and bubbly. Add Swiss cheese and brown mustard, stirring until cheese melts. Pour sauce over tortellini mixture. Toss to coat.

Spaghetti with Cream Corn Sauce

1 can cream-style corn
2 boneless chicken breasts (or same amount
    of boneless pork), cut into bite-sized pieces
2 tbsp. oil
salt to taste
pepper to taste
1 tbsp. soy sauce
spaghetti, cooked

Heat oil in a skillet. Cook meat in oil until done, adding salt to taste. Add corn and enough water to keep sauce from being too concentrated; boil. Add salt, pepper, and soy sauce to taste. Serve over cooked spaghetti.

Italian Pasta and Peas

1/4 c. olive oil
pinches of basil, mint, and oregano
1 large clove garlic, chopped
2 tsp. tomato paste
1 can (14 oz.) Italian plum tomatoes, peeled
1 can (8 oz.) sweet peas
1 lb. small pasta shells (Ditalini or macaroni)
fresh Romano or Parmesan cheese, grated

In skillet, heat oil and sauté onion and garlic until transparent. Add tomato paste and mix well. Add tomatoes with their liquid, breaking up tomatoes with a fork. Add peas and their liquid. Let simmer. Season to taste with basil, mint, and oregano.

Cook pasta according to package directions. Drain, but do not rinse. Add pasta to sauce and stir well. Serve in bowls. Top each serving with cheese.

Microwave Mexican Manicotti

1/2 lb. lean ground beef, browned and drained
1 c. refried beans
1 tsp. dried oregano, crushed
1/2 tsp. ground cumin
10 manicotti shells
1 1/4 c. water
1 jar (8 oz.) picante sauce
1 carton (8 oz.) sour cream (optional)
1/4 c. green onions, chopped
1/4 c. black olives, sliced
1/2 c. Monterey Jack cheese, shredded

Combine ground beef, refried beans, oregano, and cumin; mix well. Fill uncooked manicotti shells with meat mixture. Arrange in 10x6x2-inch baking dish.

Combine water and picante sauce; pour over stuffed shells. Cover with vented plastic wrap. Cook in microwave on high for 10 minutes, giving dish a half-turn once. Turn shells over using tongs. Cover and cook at medium power for 17-19 minutes or until pasta is tender, giving dish a half-turn once.

Combine sour cream, green onions, and olives. Spoon mixture along center of casserole; top with cheese. Cook, uncovered, at high power for 3-5 minutes or until cheese melts.

Cheese Manicotti

8 manicotti shells
2 c. small curd cottage cheese
1 pkg. (3 oz.) cream cheese, softened
1/2 c. Parmesan cheese, grated
1/4 c. parsley, chopped
1 egg, slightly beaten
1 green onion, sliced
1/8 tsp. salt
1 jar (15 oz.) marinara sauce

Cook manicotti shells in boiling water until barely cooked. Rinse with cold water; drain.

Combine cottage cheese, cream cheese, 1/4 cup Parmesan cheese, parsley, egg, onion, and salt; mix well. Fill shells with this mixture.

Arrange shells in lightly oiled baking dish; cover with marinara sauce and remaining Parmesan cheese. Bake for 25-30 minutes at 350°F.

Angel Hair Pasta With Pimiento

1 jar (4 oz.) sliced pimientos, undrained
1/4 lb. fresh angel hair pasta
2 tbsp. Parmesan cheese, grated
1 tbsp. chives, chopped
1 tsp. olive oil
dash of garlic powder

Drain pimientos, reserving 1 teaspoon juice; set aside. Break pasta into thirds; cook in boiling water for 30 seconds or until tender but still firm. Drain well; place in a warm serving bowl with pimientos, reserved pimiento juice, cheese, chives, olive oil, and garlic powder. Toss well to coat. Serve.

Cheddar Pasta and Vegetables

2 medium carrots, sliced
1 lb. Rotini pasta
1 c. broccoli florets
2 medium green peppers, chopped
1 can (10 3/4 oz.) cream of celery soup
1/2 c. cheddar cheese, shredded
1/2 c. 2% milk
1 tsp. brown spicy mustard

Put pasta water on to boil. When it is boiling, add sliced carrots; cook for five minutes. Add Rotini and bring to a second boil. Add broccoli florets. Cook, stirring constantly, until Rotini is done, about 10 minutes. Drain into a colander.

Return pan to stove and reduce heat to low. Add remaining ingredients. Stir together over low heat until cheese is melted. Add Rotini and vegetables. Heat through, stirring occasionally.

Green Noodles With Mushroom Sauce

6 oz. bacon, cut into small pieces
1 tbsp. oil
27 oz. fresh mushrooms, washed and sliced
8 oz. onions, peeled and sliced
8 oz. heavy cream
1 1/2 c. instant broth
salt
pepper
1 bunch basil, washed and chopped fine
2 oz. Parmesan cheese, grated
15 oz. green noodles, cooked and hot

Sauté bacon in oil. Add mushrooms and onions; sauté until all liquid is evaporated. Add cream and broth to mushroom-onion mixture. Let simmer 5 minutes; season with salt and pepper to taste. Just before serving, add basil. Serve sauce over noodles; sprinkle with Parmesan cheese.

Spicy Crab Over Pasta

1 tbsp. olive oil
2 medium-sized cloves garlic, chopped fine
1/2 medium green bell pepper, diced
1 tsp. red pepper flakes, crushed
1 can (16 oz.) salt-free whole tomatoes
1/2 c. rich, salt-free fish stock
1 tbsp. tomato paste
1 tbsp. fresh parsley, chopped fine
2 tsp. sugar
1 tsp. lemon zest, grated fine
1 bay leaf
1/2 lb. flaked crabmeat
pasta, cooked and hot

In a large skillet or saucepan over medium heat, heat to sizzling oil, garlic, bell pepper, and red pepper flakes. Add tomatoes, crushing them by hand, and stir in fish stock, tomato paste, parsley, sugar, lemon zest, and bay leaf. Simmer until mixture is thick but still liquid. Stir in crabmeat and continue simmering until sauce is thick. Serve over cooked pasta.

Beef & Pork

Blend:
To thoroughly mix two or more ingredients.

Boil:
To raise the temperature of liquid until it bubbles.
The boiling temperature of water is 212°F (or 100°C).

Orange Oriental Sesame Beef Stir-Fry

1 envelope Oriental Sesame salad dressing mix
1/2 c. oil
1/4 c. orange juice
2 tbsp. soy sauce
1 tbsp. grated orange peel
1 clove garlic
1 lb. lean boneless beef sirloin, cut into strips
vegetables (peas, carrots, etc.)
hot cooked rice

Prepare salad dressing mix with oil, juice, soy sauce, orange peel, and garlic as directed on envelope.

Heat large skillet over medium heat. Cook meat in 1 tablespoon of the prepared dressing. Add vegetables and remaining dressing; cook and stir until vegetables are tender-crisp. Serve over rice. Makes 4 servings.

Mediterranean Meatballs with Yogurt and Feta Sauce

1 lb. ground beef
1/2 c. chopped, fresh, flat-leaf parsley
1 egg
1/4 c. dry bread crumbs
2 cloves garlic, minced
1/2 tsp. salt
1/4 tsp. ground pepper
1 tbsp. extra virgin olive oil
Yogurt and Feta Sauce (recipe follows)

Mix meat, parsley, egg, crumbs, garlic, salt, and pepper. Shape into 1-inch meatballs.

Heat oil in medium skillet. Add meatballs. Cook on medium-low heat for 12–15 minutes, or until cooked through, stirring occasionally. Serve with Yogurt and Feta Sauce.

Yogurt and Feta Sauce

4 oz. feta cheese, crumbled
3/4 c. plain yogurt
2 tbsp. milk
1 clove garlic, minced
1/3 c. chopped, seeded tomato
1/3 c. chopped, seeded, and peeled cucumber
1 tsp. fresh dill, chopped fine

Place cheese, yogurt, milk, and garlic in food processor or blender; cover. Blend until smooth. Stir in tomato, cucumber, and dill.

Shepherd's Pie

1 (9-inch) pie shell
1 lb. of cooked meat, such as leftover beef, pork, or turkey roast or browned ground beef
1 c. vegetables, cooked (carrots, peas, corn, etc.)
1/2 c. chopped or pearl onions
2 cloves garlic, minced
1 c. gravy or broth (same flavor as meat)
1/2 tsp. black pepper
1 tsp. salt
mashed potatoes (leftovers are fine)
butter
cheese

Spread meat in bottom of pie shell. Cover with all ingredients except mashed potatoes, butter, and cheese. Warm mashed potatoes slightly before spreading. Spread potatoes over top of casserole and dot with butter. Bake at 350°F until potatoes are well browned. Add cheese if desired.

VARIATION: Try a vegetarian version made with just mushrooms, onions, broccoli, and carrots.

Cajun Meat Ring

1 egg, beaten
3/4 c. soft bread crumbs
1/4 c. milk
1/4 c. onion, chopped fine
1/2 tsp. garlic salt
1/2 tsp. dried thyme, crushed
1/2 tsp. hot pepper sauce
1 lb. ground beef
hot cooked rice

In a large mixing bowl, combine beaten egg, bread crumbs, milk, onion, garlic salt, thyme, and hot pepper sauce. Add ground beef. Mix well.

In a 9-inch, microwave-safe pie plate, shape the meat mixture into a 6-inch ring that is 2 inches wide. Cover with waxed paper. Cook on high for 7–9 minutes, giving the dish a quarter-turn every 3 minutes. Cook until no pink remains and meat is done (170°F). Transfer meat ring to a platter. Cover and keep warm while preparing sauce.

Sauce

1 can tomato sauce (8-oz.)
1/4 c. chopped green pepper
1/4 tsp. celery seed
hot pepper sauce

In a 2-cup microwave-safe measure, combine tomato sauce, green pepper, celery seed, and several dashes of hot pepper sauce. Cover with waxed paper. Cook on high for 3–4 minutes, stirring once. Cook until green pepper is tender. Spoon some sauce over meat ring. Serve with rice and remaining sauce.

Grilled Tangy Beef

1 can (10 3/4 oz.) tomato soup
2 tbsp. packed brown sugar
2 tbsp. lemon juice
2 tbsp. vegetable oil
1 tbsp. Worcestershire sauce
1 tsp. garlic powder
1/4 tsp. dried thyme leaves, crushed
1 1/2 lb. boneless beef sirloin steak, 3/4-inch thick

Mix soup, sugar, lemon juice, oil, Worcestershire, garlic powder, and thyme. Place steak on lightly oiled grill rack over medium-hot coals. Grill uncovered to desired doneness (allow 15 minutes for medium), turning once and brushing often with soup mixture. Heat remaining soup mixture to boiling and serve with steak.

VARIATION: Use 6 skinless, boneless chicken breast halves (about 1 1/2 lb.) instead of steak.

Chunky Beef Fritters

6 tbsp. milk
1 tbsp. all-purpose flour
3 large eggs, beaten
1 1/2 c. self-rising flour
4 tsp. salt
1/4 tsp. pepper
2 lb. roast beef, cut into 3/4-inch pieces

Combine milk and all-purpose flour; stir in eggs. Combine self-rising flour, salt, and pepper. Dip roast beef chunks into egg mixture, then dredge in flour mixture. Fry in hot fat until browned and heated through. Drain and serve hot with assorted vegetable sticks.

Beef and Vegetable Stir-Fry

3/4 lb. beef round steak, boneless
1 tsp. oil
1/2 c. sliced carrots
1/2 c. sliced celery
1/2 c. sliced onion
1 tbsp. soy sauce
1/8 tsp. garlic powder
dash pepper
2 c. zucchini, cut into thin strips
1 tbsp. cornstarch
1/4 c. water

Trim all fat from steak. Slice steak across the grain into thin strips about 1/8–inch wide and 3 inches long. (Partially frozen meat is easier to slice).

Heat oil in frying pan. Add beef strips and stir-fry over high heat, turning pieces constantly, until beef is no longer red (about 3–4 minutes).

Reduce heat. Add carrots, celery, onion, and seasonings. Cover and cook until carrots are slightly tender (3–5 minutes).

Add zucchini; cook until vegetables are tender-crisp (3–4 minutes). Mix cornstarch and water until smooth; add slowly to beef mixture, stirring constantly.

Cook until mixture is thickened and vegetables are coated with a thin glaze.

Individual Meatloaves

1 1/2 lb. ground beef
1 c. soft bread crumbs
3/4 c. milk
1/4 c. chopped onion
1 egg
1 tbsp. Worcestershire sauce
1 tsp. salt
1/2 tsp. dry mustard
1/4 tsp. pepper
1/4 tsp. ground sage
barbecue sauce

Mix all ingredients except barbecue sauce. Divide mixture into 6 parts; shape into loaves. Arrange on microwave rack in baking dish. Spread each loaf with about 1 teaspoon barbecue sauce.

Cover with waxed paper; place on microwave turntable and microwave on high for 12–14 minutes or until meatloaves are done.

Note: Loaves can be refrigerated before microwaving, if covered, up to 24 hours.

At serving time, cover with waxed paper and microwave as above. Or, microwave all meatloaves, then cool and wrap individually for freezer storage.

Frozen loaves can be defrosted and reheated in the microwave as needed.

Spicy Tomato Meatballs

Meatballs

1 lb. ground beef
1/2 c. dry bread crumbs
1/4 c. water
1/4 c. shredded cheddar cheese
1/4 c. chopped onion
1 tbsp. finely chopped green chiles
1 egg
1 tsp. salt
1/4 tsp. pepper
Spicy Tomato Sauce (recipe follows)

In 1 1/2-quart casserole, mix all ingredients for meatballs. Shape mixture by teaspoonfuls into 1-inch balls. Arrange in baking dish. Cover loosely and microwave on high for 3 minutes; rearrange meatballs. Cover and microwave until no longer pink inside, about 3–5 minutes more; drain.

Spicy Tomato Sauce

1 can (8 oz.) tomato sauce
3/4 c. finely chopped tomato
2 cloves garlic, finely chopped
1 tbsp. lemon juice
1/8 tsp. ground cumin
1/8 tsp. salt

Mix all ingredients. Gently stir meatballs into sauce until coated. Cover tightly and microwave on high, stirring every 5 minutes, until hot and bubbly, 12–15 minutes.

Makes 4 servings.

Oven-Baked Pork Chops

1 egg, beaten
2 tbsp. soy sauce
1 tbsp. dry sherry or water
1/4 tsp. ground ginger
1/4 tsp. garlic powder
4 lean pork chops
dry bread crumbs to coat

Beat together egg, soy sauce, and sherry with ginger and garlic powder. Dip chops in egg mixture; coat evenly with bread crumbs. Arrange chops in a single layer in baking dish sprayed with nonstick vegetable oil. Bake at 350°F for 30 minutes. Turn and bake until tender, about 20 minutes more.

Pork and Sweet Potato Skillet

4 thin-cut pork chops (about 1 lb.)
1 c. apple juice, divided
1 medium onion, cut in 1/4-inch slices
1 tbsp. flour
1/8 tsp. ground allspice
1/8 tsp. salt
1 can (17 oz.) sweet potatoes

Trim fat from chops. Brown on both sides in hot frying pan. Add 3/4 cup of apple juice. Top with onion slices. Cover and cook 5 minutes at reduced heat. Mix flour and seasonings. Stir into remaining apple juice and add all to liquid in pan. Arrange sweet potatoes around and over chops. Spoon sauce over potatoes. Cover and cook until potatoes are hot and chops are done, about ten minutes more.

Pork Chop Dinner

2 tsp. olive oil
4 pork chops
1 can chicken broth
1 onion, chopped
2 cloves garlic, chopped

Heat oil in frying pan until hot. Brown pork chops on both sides. Add chicken broth, onions, and garlic. Simmer on low for about 1 hour or until chops are tender but not dried out.

Hot Ham and Cheese Sandwiches

Dijon mustard
6 slices rye or pumpernickel bread
6 slices deli ham
3 apples or pears, cored and sliced thin
6 slices Swiss or cheddar cheese

Spread mustard on bread. Top with ham slices. Lay fruit slices over ham and top with a slice of cheese. Cook under a hot broiler (or in a toaster oven) until cheese melts and bubbles.

Makes 6 servings.

Taco Pie

1 lb. ground beef
1 pkg. taco seasoning
1 pkg. corn muffin mix (an egg and milk will probably be needed with this)
1 c. shredded cheddar cheese

In a large skillet, brown meat. Drain off excess grease. Add taco seasoning mix according to directions on package. Bring meat mixture to a simmer.

Preheat oven to 400°F. Spray a baking dish with cooking spray.

In a bowl, mix corn muffin mix according to package directions. Place meat mixture in baking dish, sprinkle with cheese, and pour corn muffin mix over top. Bake for 10–15 minutes, or until corn bread is done.

Mexican Pork Chops and Beans

1 oven cooking bag, large size
2 tbsp. flour
1 c. thick and chunky salsa
2 tbsp. lime juice
3/4 tsp. chili powder
1/2 tsp. garlic powder
4 pork chops, 1/2-inch thick, fat trimmed off
1 can (16 oz.) light red kidney beans, drained
2 medium green, yellow, orange, or red sweet peppers, cubed

Preheat oven to 350°F. Shake flour in cooking bag; place in 13x9x2-inch baking pan. Add salsa, lime juice, chili powder, and garlic powder to bag. Squeeze bag to blend ingredients. Place pork chops in bag. Spoon beans and peppers around pork chops. Close bag with nylon tie; cut 6 half-inch slits in top. Bake until pork chops are tender, 35–40 minutes. Let stand in bag 5 minutes.

Makes 4 servings.

Quick Mexican Pizza

1/2 lb. lean ground beef
1 1/2 tsp. chili powder
1/2 tsp. cumin
1 c. salsa, divided
4 flour tortillas
2 c. shredded Monterey Jack cheese, divided
green pepper
onion
mushrooms

In a skillet, cook meat over medium-high heat until it browns. Drain off excess grease and stir in chili powder and cumin.

Spread 1/4 cup salsa and 1/2 cup of meat mixture on each tortilla. Top each with 1/2 cup cheese and peppers, onions, or mushrooms, as desired. Bake 8–10 minutes at 400°F or until crisp and lightly browned. Makes 4 servings.

Barbecue Meatloaf

2 lb. lean ground beef
1 1/2 c. bread crumbs
1 onion, chopped
8 oz. tomato sauce
1 large egg
1 tsp. garlic powder
1 tsp. onion powder
1 tsp. pepper
1 green pepper, chopped

Sauce:
1/2 c. water
3 tbsp. vinegar
3 tbsp. brown sugar
2 tbsp. prepared mustard
1 1/2 c. tomato sauce
2 tbsp. butter

Combine beef, bread crumbs, onion, tomato sauce, egg, seasonings, and green pepper. Mix well and place in a loaf pan.

Combine all sauce ingredients. Cook in a saucepan until butter melts. Pour sauce over meatloaf and bake at 350°F for 1 hour, basting occasionally.

Beef Stroganoff Sandwich

2 lb. ground beef
1/2 c. chopped onion
1 tsp. salt
1/2 tsp. garlic powder
1/2 tsp. ground pepper
1 loaf French bread
2 c. sour cream
2 tomatoes, seeded and diced
1 large green pepper, diced
3 c. cheddar cheese, shredded
butter

In a skillet, brown ground beef and onion. Drain. Add salt, garlic powder, and pepper.

Cut bread lengthwise in half; butter both halves and place on a baking sheet.

Remove meat mixture from heat; stir in sour cream. Spoon meat and sour cream mixture onto bread. Sprinkle with tomatoes, green pepper, and cheese.

Bake at 350°F for 20 minutes or until cheese is melted. (Bake longer for crispier bread.)

Beef With Broccoli

1 c. beef, sliced thin
salt
2 tbsp. soy sauce
1 tbsp. red wine
1/2 bunch broccoli, shredded into
   3-inch lengths
2 tbsp. sugar
3 tbsp. oil
1/2 c. water

Carefully slice beef into thin, bite-sized pieces, across grain of beef. Marinate beef in soy sauce, wine, and salt.

Place oil in wok and heat to smoking point. Quickly stir-fry beef for no more than 3 minutes. Remove beef and set aside.

Add broccoli, water, and sugar to wok; cover. Cook over medium-high heat, stirring frequently, for 6 minutes or until broccoli is cooked through. Add beef back to broccoli and stir. Place on a platter and serve.

Chili Macaroni

3/4 lb. ground beef
1 onion, chopped
1 can (14-oz.) tomatoes, diced
1 1/4 c. tomato juice
1 4-oz. can green chili peppers, diced
2 tsp. chili powder
1/2 tsp. garlic salt
1 c. elbow macaroni
1 c. frozen cut green beans
1 c. shredded cheddar cheese

Brown ground beef and onion in a large skillet; drain. Stir undrained diced tomatoes, tomato juice, chili peppers, chili powder, and garlic **salt** into meat mixture. Bring to a boil. Stir in

uncooked macaroni and green beans. Return to boiling; reduce heat. Simmer, covered, about 15 minutes or until macaroni and beans are tender. To serve, spoon into bowls; sprinkle with cheese.

Chinese Beef Stir-Fry With Vegetables

1 lb. sirloin tips, cut into 1-inch cubes
1 tbsp. dry sherry
1 tbsp. soy sauce
1 tbsp. cornstarch, divided
1/2 tsp. sugar
6 1/2 tsp. oil, divided
1/8 tsp. black pepper
2 cloves garlic, pressed
1 tbsp. oyster sauce
2 broccoli stalks, stems removed, cut into florets
1/2 c. beef broth
8 baby corn spears, drained
20 fresh snow pea pods
1 scallion with top, chopped

Combine sherry, soy sauce, 1/2 tablespoon cornstarch, sugar, 1/2 teaspoon oil, pepper, and garlic. Add sirloin and marinate for one hour at room temperature.

Heat 1 tablespoon oil in a wok over high heat. Stir-fry beef in oil until medium-rare. Remove from heat; set aside.

Combine oyster sauce and remaining cornstarch. Reheat wok with remaining oil. Add broccoli and stir-fry for 30 seconds. Add remaining vegetables and beef broth. Stir-fry for one additional minute. Add beef and continue to stir-fry for another minute. Serve over rice.

Deli In a Skillet

1 lb. corned beef, cooked and cut into pieces
1 14-oz. can sauerkraut
1 1/2 c. water
3/4 tsp. caraway seed
1 1/2 c. dry rice
1/2 c. Thousand Island salad dressing
3 oz. Swiss cheese, cut into strips

Mix corned beef, sauerkraut, water, and caraway seed in a large skillet. Bring to a full boil. Stir in rice. Pour dressing over rice and top with cheese. Cover; remove from heat. Let stand 5 minutes.

Easy Beef Roll-Ups

2 lb. beef round steak
1 1/2 lb. lean bacon
2 tsp. oil
1 envelope onion soup mix (1-1/4 oz.)
2 1/2 c. water
2 tsp. cornstarch
1/2 c. water
3 cherry tomatoes
parsley

Trim fat from steak and remove any bone. Pound with meat mallet or saucer; slice into 1x4-inch strips. Trim any excess fat from bacon. Place bacon slices on steak strips and roll up, securing with small wooden picks. Heat oil in large pan. Brown roll-ups slowly in hot oil. Remove roll-ups to pressure cooker.

Add soup mix and 2 cups water to frying pan and simmer 3 minutes, scraping particles from pan. Pour liquid over roll-ups. Cook at 10 pounds pressure for 10 minutes. Remove roll-ups to warm serving dish.

Combine cornstarch and 1/2 cup water, mixing until smooth. Add to liquid in pressure cooker and simmer, stirring constantly, 3 to 4 minutes or until thickened. Pour gravy over roll-ups. Garnish with parsley and cherry tomatoes.

Steak Diane

4 sirloin steaks (6 oz. ea.)
8 tbsp. butter, divided
4 shallots, chopped fine
2 tbsp. Worcestershire sauce
salt
pepper, freshly ground
parsley, chopped

Put steaks between pieces of waxed paper and pound to a 1/3-inch thickness.

In small saucepan, heat 2 tablespoons butter. Add shallots and cook until lightly browned. Add Worcestershire sauce and heat to bubbling. Keep sauce hot.

Brown 6 tablespoons butter in 12-inch skillet or chafing dish. Add steaks and cook for 3 minutes. Turn and cook for 2 to 3 minutes more or to desired doneness.

Transfer steaks to a serving dish and sprinkle with salt and a generous amount of freshly ground pepper.

Spread shallot sauce over steaks and sprinkle with chopped parsley.

Citrus Sirloin Strips

1/4 c. fresh lemon juice (about 2 lemons)
3 tbsp. light olive oil, divided
1 tbsp. honey
1/2 c. orange juice
1/4 tbsp. ground white pepper
1/4 c. red-wine vinegar
1/4 tsp. salt
1 clove garlic, minced
1/2 tsp. thyme
1 1/2 lb. top sirloin steak, trimmed of excess fat
1 red onion, sliced and separated into rings
5 medium mushrooms, sliced thin
1 pkg. Romaine lettuce leaves, torn
1 artichoke
orange and lemon slices

In shallow dish, combine marinade ingredients: lemon juice, 2 tablespoons oil, honey, orange juice, white pepper, vinegar, salt, garlic, and thyme. Refrigerate 1/4 cup marinade to toss with vegetables.

Add beef to marinade, turning once to coat. Cover; marinate in refrigerator 1 hour. Remove beef from marinade and place in shallow baking pan. Pour any leftover marinade over beef. Bake at 450°F for 10 to 15 minutes or to desired doneness.

Meanwhile, sauté onion and mushrooms in remaining oil for 2 to 3 minutes. In small saucepan, heat reserved marinade for 2 to 3 minutes or until warmed. Pour in large bowl; toss in onions and mushrooms. Arrange lettuce leaves on a serving platter. Carve steak diagonally into thin slices; fan onto lettuce leaves.

Place onion rings and mushrooms alongside and on top of beef slices. Pour any remaining marinade (from vegetable toss) over beef. Place artichoke on one side of platter with lemon and orange slices around it, forming a flower effect. Serve.

Grilled Beef Kabobs

1/4 c. lemon juice
2 tbsp. Worcestershire sauce
3 tbsp. corn oil
1/3 c. soy sauce
2 tbsp. yellow mustard
1 clove garlic, minced
1 1/2 lb. lean, boneless round steak, cut into
  1-inch chunks
1 large green pepper, cut into 8 pieces
4 oz. fresh mushrooms
8 cherry tomatoes
1 very large onion, cut into 8 pieces

Make marinade: combine lemon juice, Worcestershire sauce, oil, soy sauce, mustard, and garlic. Add beef chunks to marinade and cover; marinate in refrigerator for 12 hours or more.

Remove beef cubes from marinade, reserving marinade. On 4 medium or long skewers, alternate pieces of meat and vegetables.

Grill for about 15 minutes over hot coals, turning skewers regularly and basting occasionally with reserved marinade. (Allow 5 to 10 minutes more for well-done meat.) Serve hot.

Casseroles & Side Dishes

Chop:
To cut into bite-sized pieces.

Combine:
To stir together two or more ingredients.

Macaroni and Cheese Southern Style

1 pkg. (7 1/4 oz.) macaroni and cheese dinner
  (milk and butter will be needed with this)
1 c. cooked ham, cubed
1 c. frozen green peas, cooked and drained
1/2 tsp. mustard

Prepare macaroni and cheese dinner as directed on package. Stir in remaining ingredients.

Chicken-Flavored Rice

2 tbsp. oil
1/2 c. shallots, chopped fine
2 tbsp. garlic, chopped fine
1 3/4 c. long–grain rice
1 tsp. salt
2 c. chicken stock

Heat oil over medium heat. Add shallots and garlic. Sauté until soft, translucent, and fragrant. Add rice and salt; sauté for 3 minutes. Add chicken stock and bring to a boil. Stir once to loosen rice from bottom of pan. Boil until surface of rice appears dry and craters form on surface. Cover, reduce heat to low, and simmer for 20 minutes. Remove pan from heat and let rice sit, covered, for 10 minutes before serving.

Hawaiian Sweet Potatoes

4–5 medium sweet potatoes
1/2 c. pineapple preserves
2 tbsp. butter

Boil sweet potatoes in their jackets until tender, about 25 minutes. Let cool, then peel and cut into 1/2-inch thick slices.

In a large skillet, melt pineapple preserves and butter. Add sweet potatoes to skillet. Cook gently; tossing lightly until sweet potatoes are glazed.

Honey Roast Potatoes

2 medium potatoes, peeled
2 tbsp. butter
1/4 tsp. salt
1/4 c. honey

Add potatoes to a pan of cold water, bring to a boil. Drain immediately. Place potatoes in baking dish. Add butter and sprinkle with salt. Bake at 350°F for 20 minutes. Baste with honey and bake additional 20 minutes, or until tender. Serve with any roast meat.

Cheesy Potatoes

4 medium baking potatoes
1/3 to 1/2 c. milk
1/4 c. butter, softened
1/2 tsp. salt
dash of pepper
1/4 c. cheddar cheese, shredded

Scrub whole potatoes, pierce with a fork, then microwave on high for 11–13 minutes, or until almost done. Wrap in towel until cool, about 5 minutes or longer. Cut a thin slice from the top of each potato. Scoop out the insides, leaving a thin shell. Mash potato insides until no lumps remain. Add a small amount of milk, beating after each addition. (Amount of milk needed will depend on the type of potatoes.) Add butter, salt, and pepper; beat vigorously until light and fluffy. Stir in cheese. Fill potato shells. Sprinkle with cooked bacon bits or chopped chives, if desired.

Southern Summer Squash

1 1/2 lb. yellow squash
2 tbsp. plus 2 tsp. butter
2 egg whites
1 tbsp. minced onion flakes
3 tbsp. bread crumbs, divided

Preheat oven to 350°F. Wash and slice squash and put in pan of water, cooking until soft; drain. In a large bowl, mash squash. Add 2 tablespoons of butter, egg whites, onion flakes, and 1 1/2 tablespoons of bread crumbs. Mix well. Pour mixture into a greased pan. Dot with the 2 teaspoons of butter and sprinkle top with remaining bread crumbs. Bake for 45 minutes.

Cheddar Chowder

2 c. diced potatoes
1/2 c. diced carrots
1/2 c. diced celery
1/4 c. chopped onion
1 tsp. salt
1/4 tsp. pepper
2 c. water
White Sauce (recipe follows)

Mix all ingredients except White Sauce and bring to a boil. Boil for 10–12 minutes while making the White Sauce.

White Sauce
1/4 c. butter
1/4 c. flour
2 c. milk
2 c. grated cheddar cheese
1 c. cubed ham

Melt butter in a saucepan and add flour to make a paste. Add milk and stir constantly over low to medium heat until mixture thickens. Remove from heat and add cheese.

Pour sauce into vegetables (do not drain water from vegetables) and then add ham. Heat thoroughly and serve with a salad and bread.

Hot Potato Casserole

1 1/2 lb. potatoes
2 oz. butter
1 onion, chopped
1/3 c. sour cream
2 tbsp. milk
salt and pepper
paprika

Peel and chop potatoes. Cook in boiling, salted water until tender; drain. Mash well. Melt butter in pan. Add onion, and cook until transparent. Add to potatoes along with sour cream and milk. Mix until smooth. Season with salt and pepper. Spoon potato mixture into oven-proof dish; sprinkle with paprika. Bake at 350°F for 15 minutes.

Note: Leftover casserole is delicious cut into squares and fried with bacon for breakfast!

Mexican Corn Casserole

1 pkg. Mexican corn bread mix
4 eggs
2 c. grated sharp cheddar cheese
1 small jar diced pimientos
1/4 c. oil
3 cans cream-style corn
2 sliced or chopped jalapeños (optional)

Mix all ingredients in a large bowl. Pour into greased casserole dish. Bake uncovered at 350°F until just set and lightly browned on top. May be served hot or cold.

French Fries Casserole

1 small onion
1 lb. ground beef, browned and drained
1 tsp. hot sauce
salt and pepper
1 can cheddar cheese soup
1 can cream of celery soup
1 pkg. frozen french fries

Dice onion and mix with ground beef, hot sauce, and salt and pepper to taste. Press into the bottom of a 9x9-inch pan. Mix two cans of soup (do NOT dilute). Spread mixture over meat. Cover entire surface generously with frozen french fries.

Bake at 350°F for 40 minutes, or until done— fries should be golden and crispy.

Smoked Sausage Casserole

1 tsp. cooking oil
1 small onion, chopped fine
1 can (14 oz.) tomatoes
salt and pepper
1 tsp. sugar
1 tsp. oregano
dash of Worcestershire sauce
1 large smoked sausage, chopped

Put cooking oil in saucepan. Add chopped onion and fry gently until soft (5–10 minutes). Add tomatoes, chopping while stirring. Add salt, pepper, sugar, oregano, and Worcestershire sauce. Add sausage and cook on low heat for 10 minutes, stirring occasionally.

Serve over noodles or pasta.

Chicken Noodle Casserole

1 can (10 3/4 oz.) cream of chicken soup
1/2 c. milk
1/8 tsp. pepper
1/3 c. grated Parmesan cheese
2 c. cooked chicken or turkey, cubed
3 c. medium egg noodles, cooked
chopped fresh parsley for garnish

In a large saucepan, mix soup, milk, pepper, cheese, chicken, and noodles. Heat through over medium heat, stirring occasionally. Garnish with parsley.

TIP: For 2 cups of cubed, cooked chicken:
Cook 1 pound skinless, boneless chicken breasts, cubed, in a saucepan with 4 cups boiling water over medium heat for 5 minutes, or until chicken is no longer pink.
—Or—Place chicken in a 2-quart, microwave-safe baking dish and cover with waxed paper. Microwave on high for 8 minutes, or until chicken is no longer pink. Cut into cubes.

Tuna Casserole

8 slices bread
5 tbsp. butter, melted, divided
1/2 lb. cheddar cheese, grated
1 tbsp. flour
1 can tuna, drained
1 can green peas, drained
1 tomato, sliced

Cut bread slices into 1/2-inch squares. Pour 4 tablespoons melted butter over bread and mix in cheese. In a saucepan over low heat, mix 1 tablespoon butter with flour to make a thick white sauce. Stir tuna into white sauce. Line a 9-inch baking dish with bread and cheese mixture. Pour tuna over top; add peas. Add a layer of sliced tomatoes; sprinkle with remaining bread and cheese mixture. Bake at 375°F until cheese melts.

Super Easy Tuna Casserole

1 can (10 3/4 oz.) condensed cream
  of mushroom soup
1 1/2 c. milk
1 c. frozen peas
1 1/2 c. instant rice
2 cans (6 1/8 oz. ea.) tuna, drained and flaked
1 c. (4 oz.) cheddar cheese, shredded

Bring soup, milk, and peas to a boil in a medium
saucepan. Stir in rice and tuna. Spoon into a 2-
quart casserole. Sprinkle with cheese. Bake at
375°F for 20 minutes or until thoroughly heated.

Makes 6 servings.

Wild Rice and Turkey Casserole

1 box wild rice
1 small onion, diced
1/2 c. chopped celery
1 can cream of mushroom soup
1/3 c. white wine
1/2 c. sour cream
1 tsp. curry powder
1 tbsp. black pepper
2 c. cubed turkey

Prepare rice according to package directions.

Sauté onion and celery until tender in pan
coated with cooking spray. Mix in soup, wine,
sour cream, and spices. Bring to a boil. Add
turkey. Pour into a 3-quart casserole dish. Add
cooked rice. Bake at 350°F, uncovered, for 30–
35 minutes.

Hearty Ham and Noodle Casserole

1 3/4 c. medium noodles
1 can (10 3/4 oz.) condensed cheddar cheese soup
1/2 c. milk
1/2 c. sour cream
1/2 c. celery, sliced thin
1 jar (2 1/2 oz.) sliced mushrooms, drained
2 tbsp. chopped pimiento
1 tsp. dried parsley flakes
1 tsp. dried minced onion
2 c. diced cooked ham
1/4 c. dry bread crumbs
1 tbsp. butter, melted

Cook noodles according to package directions;
drain. In a 2-quart, microwave-safe casserole dish,
combine soup, milk, and sour cream. Stir in celery,
mushrooms, pimiento, parsley flakes, and onion.
Stir in cooked noodles and meat.

Microwave, uncovered, on high for 10–12 minutes,
or until hot, stirring twice. Combine bread crumbs
and margarine; sprinkle over casserole. Cook on
high for 30 seconds more. Makes 4–5 servings.

Classic Guacamole

4 avocados, seeded and peeled
2 tbsp. lemon juice
1 clove garlic, crushed
1 tomato, chopped fine
1/4 c. onion, chopped fine
1/4 tsp. ground cumin
3–4 drops hot pepper sauce
tortilla chips

Using a fork, mash avocado with lemon juice and
garlic. Stir in remaining ingredients to blend. Garnish as desired and serve with tortilla chips.

Spicy Nachos Supreme

1 can (8 oz.) tomato sauce
1 can (4 oz.) diced green chilies
1/2 c. chopped green bell pepper
1 green onion, sliced
1/4 tsp. hot pepper sauce
1 bag (10 oz.) tortilla chips
2 c. shredded cheddar cheese
1 avocado
1 tsp. lemon juice
1/2 c. sour cream
jalapeño pepper slices (optional)

Combine tomato sauce, chilies, green pepper, green onion, and hot pepper sauce in bowl; let stand 15 minutes. Place tortilla chips in shallow, 8x10-inch baking dish. Pour sauce over chips; sprinkle grated cheese over all. Broil nachos 3 minutes or until cheese melts. Just before serving, seed, peel, and mash avocado. Stir in lemon juice. Spoon avocado mixture and sour cream on hot nachos and top with jalapeño slices. Serve immediately.

Beef and Rice Casserole

1 tbsp. butter
1 c. onion, chopped
1 tsp. fresh garlic, minced
1/2 lb. ground beef
1 can broccoli-cheese soup
1/2 c. milk
salt and pepper to taste
10 oz. chopped broccoli
3/4 c. rice, cooked
seasoned bread crumbs (optional)
Parmesan cheese (optional)

Preheat oven to 350° F. Sauté onions and garlic in butter until onions are just tender. Add ground beef and brown. Cook onions and ground beef about 7 minutes. Drain fat and return to medium heat.

Combine soup and milk; stir until creamy. Add salt and pepper to taste. Add soup mixture, rice, and broccoli to ground beef, tossing carefully. Pour into a 9x9-inch casserole dish. Top with seasoned bread crumbs and Parmesan cheese, if desired. Bake about 35 minutes.

Beef, Brown Rice, and Feta Casserole

6 dried mushrooms
1/2 c. hot water
1 onion, chopped
1 tbsp. oil
1 1/2 c. canned tomatoes
1 clove garlic, minced
pepper, freshly ground
2 c. brown rice, cooked
1 1/2 c. beef chunks, cooked
3 oz. feta cheese, crumbled
6 pitted black olives
2 tbsp. Parmesan cheese

Put dried mushrooms in water and let stand 20 minutes.

Meanwhile, sauté onion in oil for 5 minutes. Add tomatoes and garlic; cook uncovered over low heat for about 10 minutes. Season with pepper to taste.

Remove tough stems from rehydrated mushrooms. Quarter any large mushrooms. Add mushrooms and their soaking liquid to onion-tomato mixture. Cook for another 5 minutes.

Preheat oven to 400° F. Line bottom of 1 1/2-quart casserole with 1 cup rice. Add cooked beef. Strew feta cheese, olives, and half of sauce over top. Add remaining rice and rest of sauce. Sprinkle with Parmesan and bake for 20 minutes.

Dried Beef And Noodle Casserole

4 oz. dried beef, snipped
2 c. water
1 small onion, chopped
2 c. uncooked noodles
1 can cream of mushroom soup
1/2 c. milk
1 tsp. dried parsley flakes
4 oz. (1 c.) cheddar cheese, shredded

Place dried beef and 1 cup water water in microwaveable 2-quart casserole; cover. Microwave on high to boiling, about 2-3 minutes; drain. Stir in remaining water, onion, noodles, soup, milk, and parsley flakes. Cover and microwave 10 minutes; stir. Replace cover and microwave until noodles are tender, about 5-6 minutes more. Stir in cheese. Replace cover and microwave until melted, about 2-3 minutes. Let stand 5 minutes before serving.

Auntie's Chicken Casserole

8 oz. macaroni
1/2 lb. processed American cheese
4 eggs, hard boiled and chopped
1 can cream of mushroom soup
2 c. chicken, cooked and chopped
1 can cream of chicken soup
2 c. milk

Combine all ingredients in a casserole dish. Cover and refrigerate overnight.

Remove 1 hour before cooking. Bake 1 hour at 350°F.

Asparagus Ham Quiche

2 pkg. (10 oz. ea.) frozen cut asparagus, thawed
1 lb. ham, cooked and chopped
2 c. (8 oz.) Swiss cheese, shredded
1/2 c. onion, chopped
6 eggs
2 c. milk
1 1/2 c. buttermilk baking mix
2 tbsp. dried vegetable flakes
1/4 tsp. pepper

In two greased 9-inch pie plates, layer asparagus, ham, cheese, and onion. In a bowl, beat eggs. Add remaining ingredients and mix well. Divide in half and pour over asparagus mixture in each pie plate. Bake at 375° F for 30 minutes or until a knife inserted near the center comes out clean.

Broccoli-Rice Casserole

1 box frozen broccoli
1 1/2 c. onions, sautéed
2 c. instant rice
1 16-oz. jar microwaveable cheese sauce
2 cans cream of mushroom soup

Combine all ingredients and bake at 350°F for approximately 1 hour.

Baked Green Tomatoes

15 large green tomatoes, cut in half
salt and pepper
2 c. brown sugar
3 c. butter crackers, coarsely crumbled
2 sticks butter

Coat a shallow casserole with cooking spray. Arrange tomatoes in dish and season with salt and pepper. Spread each tomato half with a tablespoon of sugar. Cover with crumbs and dot with butter. Bake at 350°F until tender but still firm, about 30-40 minutes.

Beef-Corn Faux Casserole

4 tbsp. oil
18 oz. beef roast (not too lean), cubed
1 clove garlic, chopped fine
2 onions, chopped fine
1 red pepper, diced
1 green pepper, diced
9 oz. carrots, diced
1 leek, diced
2 qt. clear broth
2 c. rice
2 cans whole-kernel corn
2 tsp. paprika
1/2 tsp. salt
1 tsp. pepper
1 bunch parsley, chopped

Heat oil in a big pot; brown meat in oil. Add garlic, onions, chopped peppers, carrots, and leek to meat and sauté. Add broth and bring to a boil. Add rice and let simmer for 20 minutes. Add corn and let simmer for another 10 minutes. Season with paprika, salt, and pepper. Add parsley. Serve with a hearty bread.

Bacon-Potato Pie

1 lb. lean bacon, thick-sliced, cut into
   squares, fried and drained
1 onion, minced
1 lb. baking potatoes, peeled and grated
1/2 lb. cheddar cheese, grated
8 eggs

Butter a 9x13-inch shallow baking dish. Preheat oven to 350° F.

Beat eggs in a large bowl. Add all other ingredients and stir. Pour mixture into baking dish and bake for about 45 minutes or until eggs are cooked. Serve hot, warm, or at room temperature.

Spaghetti Casserole

1 lb. hamburger
2 onions, chopped
2 celery stalks, chopped
1 green pepper, chopped
1 c. tomatoes
1 pkg. spaghetti or other pasta
2 tsp. blue cheese, crumbled
1/4 c. cheese, grated

Preheat oven to 350°F.

Brown hamburger, stirring until light brown and crumbly; drain. Add onions, celery, and green pepper. Cook for 3 minutes. Add tomatoes and simmer a few minutes more. Add salt and pepper.

Prepare pasta according to package directions; drain. In buttered 2-quart casserole, combine pasta, sauce, and blue cheese. Sprinkle grated cheese on top. Bake at 350°F for 20 minutes.

Rice and Sour Cream Casserole

3/4 lb. Monterey Jack Cheese, cut into
   1/8-inch thick strips
3 c. sour cream
2 cans green chilies, diced
salt and pepper to taste
3 c. rice, cooked
1/2 c. cheddar cheese, grated

Cut Jack cheese into strips about 1/8–inch thick. Thoroughly mix sour cream and chilies. Grease (with butter or cooking spray) a 1 1/2-quart casserole. Season rice with salt and pepper.

Layer rice, sour cream mixture, and cheese strips; continue layering in that order, finishing with a layer of rice. Bake in 350°F oven for 25 minutes. Sprinkle grated cheddar over rice and continue baking until cheese melts, about 5 minutes more.

Desserts

Fry:
To cook in hot oil that does not completely cover the
food over medium to high heat.

Garnish:
To decorate food with colorful pieces, such as parsley.

One-Bowl Macaroons

2 2/3 c. shredded coconut
2/3 c. sweetened condensed milk
1 tsp. vanilla

Heat oven to 350°F. Mix coconut, milk, and vanilla in large bowl. Drop by teaspoonfuls about 1 inch apart onto well-greased cookie sheets, pressing down ends of coconut with back of spoon.

Bake 10–12 minutes or until golden brown. Immediately remove from cookie sheets. Cool on wire racks.

Strawberry Pudding with Cream

1 1/2 lb. fresh strawberries
2 c. water
1/2 c. sugar
3 tbsp. cornstarch
2 tbsp. cold water
1 pt. light cream
slivered almonds

Wash and drain berries. There should be 2 1/2 cups of berries. Add 2 cups of water and cook until berries are soft. Add sugar.

In a separate bowl, mix cornstarch and 2 tablespoons cold water. Add a small amount of berry juice; mix well. Add cornstarch mixture to berry mixture. Cook, stirring constantly, until pudding thickens. Reduce heat and cook 10 minutes. Pour into serving dish. Let stand until cold. Decorate with slivered almonds. Serve with a pitcher of cream.

Quick Banana Pudding

3 small boxes instant vanilla pudding mix
5 c. cold milk
12 oz. whipped topping, divided
8 oz. sour cream
1 large box vanilla wafers
5–6 large bananas

Mix pudding mix with milk. Fold in half of whipped topping and sour cream. In a large bowl, layer wafers, bananas, and pudding mixture. Top with remaining whipped topping. Refrigerate.

Bread Pudding

4 c. bread cubes (lightly packed into cup,
    about 4–5 slices)
1/2 c. brown sugar, firmly packed
1/4 tsp. salt
1/2 c. raisins
2 c. milk
1/4 c. butter
2 eggs

Spread bread cubes evenly in an 8-inch, round, microwave-safe dish. Sprinkle evenly with brown sugar, salt, and then raisins.

Microwave butter and milk on high for 4 minutes or until butter is melted and milk is warm. Rapidly stir in eggs with a fork and mix well. Pour over bread cubes in dish.

Microwave at medium-high for 9–12 minutes, rotating dish 1/4 turn after 6 minutes. When cooked, center may still be slightly soft, but it will set as pudding cools. Serve warm or chilled.

Mousse In a Flash

1 1/2 c. cold milk
1 pkg. (4-serving size) instant chocolate
    pudding mix
1 1/2 c. whipped topping, divided
fresh raspberries (optional)
mint leaves (optional)

Pour milk into a large bowl. Add pudding mix. Beat with a wire whisk for 2 minutes. Stir in 1 cup of whipped topping. Spoon into a serving bowl or individual dessert dishes. Refrigerate until ready to serve. Garnish with remaining whipped topping. Top with fresh raspberries and mint leaves, if desired.

Microwave Baked Apples

4 large baking apples, cored
1/2 c. syrup
3 tbsp. butter or margarine, melted
1/2 tsp. ground cinnamon

Cut a thin slice off the bottom of each apple to form a flat surface. Place apples in a microwave-safe casserole dish. Mix syrup, butter, and cinnamon in a small bowl. Spoon into center of apples. Cover loosely with waxed paper. Microwave on high for 10 minutes or until apples are tender, rotating dish halfway through cooking time.

Cherry Crisp

1 can cherry pie filling
2 tbsp. lemon juice
1 tsp. almond flavoring
1 stick margarine
1 box white cake mix
1/2 c. chopped walnuts

Mix cherry pie filling, lemon juice, and almond flavoring. Pour into a 9-inch baking pan. Melt margarine; mix with dry cake mix and walnuts. Sprinkle over cherry mixture. Bake at 350°F for 30 minutes, or until slightly brown on top.

Note: Try using chocolate cake mix for a black forest taste.

Blueberry Cobbler

Biscuit Topping
1 c. all-purpose flour
2 tbsp. sugar
1 1/2 tsp. baking powder
1/4 tsp. salt
1/4 c. butter
1/4 c. milk
1 egg, slightly beaten

Sift together flour, sugar, baking powder, and salt. Cut in butter until you have a coarse crumb consistency. In a separate bowl, combine milk and slightly beaten egg. Add all at once to dry ingredients, stirring just until moistened. Set aside.

Fruit Filling
3 c. blueberries
1/2 c. sugar
1 tbsp. quick cooking tapioca
1/2 c. water
1 tbsp. butter

Combine blueberries, sugar, tapioca, and water in a saucepan. Let stand 5 minutes. Cook and stir until slightly thickened and bubbly (about 5 minutes). Stir in butter.

Pour filling into an 8-inch round baking dish. Immediately spoon on biscuit topping in 6 mounds. Bake at 400°F for 20–25 minutes. Serve warm with cream or ice cream.

Banana Cream Pie

3/4 c. sugar
1/3 c. all-purpose flour
3 tbsp. cornstarch
1/4 tsp. salt
2 c. milk
3 egg yolks, slightly beaten
2 tbsp. butter
1 tsp. vanilla
1 (9-inch) pastry shell, baked and cooked
3–4 bananas
whipped cream

Combine sugar, flour, cornstarch, and salt in a saucepan. Add milk gradually. Cook, stirring constantly, over medium heat until bubbly. Cook and stir an additional 2 minutes, then remove from burner.

Stir a small amount of hot mixture into egg yolks, then immediately add the entire egg yolk mixture to hot mixture and cook for 2 minutes, stirring constantly. Remove from heat. Add butter and vanilla; stir until smooth. Slice 3–4 bananas into cooled pastry shell. Top with pudding mixture. Bake at 350°F for 12–15 minutes. Cool. Top with whipped cream.

Kentucky Derby Pie

1/2 c. margarine, melted
1 c. sugar
1/2 c. flour
2 eggs, slightly beaten
1 tsp. vanilla
3/4 c. pecan halves or pieces
3/4 c. chocolate chips
1 (9-inch) pie crust, unbaked

Mix ingredients in order given. Pour into pie crust. Bake at 350°F for 30 minutes.

Dirt Pie

1 c. cold milk
1 pkg (4 oz.) instant chocolate pudding mix
1 container (8 oz.) whipped topping
20 chocolate sandwich cookies, crushed
1 1/2 cups "rocks" (granola chunks, chocolate chips, peanut butter chips, chopped peanuts, or any combination of these)
1 graham cracker pie crust

Pour milk into medium bowl. Add pudding mix. Beat with wire whisk until well blended. Let stand 5 minutes. Fold in whipped topping. Stir 1 cup of cookies and all of the "rocks" into pudding mix. Spoon into pie crust. Sprinkle with remaining cookies. Freeze until firm, about 4 hours.

Peach Cobbler

Dough
2 c. biscuit mix
1/2 c. milk
2 tsp. sugar

Filling
3 c. peaches, peeled and sliced (apples, pears, or plums may be used instead)
2/3 c. sugar
1 tsp. flour
1 tsp. cinnamon, divided
1/2 tsp. nutmeg
2 tbsp. butter

Preheat oven to 425°F. Mix filling ingredients in pot; place on medium heat and allow to boil. Put hot fruit in bottom of greased casserole dish. Sprinkle with half of cinnamon and nutmeg. Dot with 1 tablespoon butter. Mix dough ingredients in separate bowl; form into ball. Roll out dough. Cover filling with rolled dough. Dot dough with 1 tablespoon butter and sprinkle with 1/2 teaspoon cinnamon. Bake 30 minutes at 425°F.

Orange Freeze Pie

1 pkg. (3 oz.) orange–flavored gelatin
2/3 c. boiling orange juice
1 c. vanilla ice cream, softened
1 can (11 oz.) mandarin oranges, drained
1 c. whipped topping, thawed
1 deep–dish pie shell, baked

Dissolve gelatin in boiling orange juice. Add ice cream by spoonfuls, blending until dissolved. Chill until slightly thickened. Stir in mandarin oranges. Fold in whipped topping. Pour into pie shell. Freeze until firm, about 2 hours. Remove from freezer 15 minutes before serving.

American Key Lime Pie

1 tbsp. (1 env.) unflavored gelatin
1 c. sugar, divided
1/4 tsp. salt
4 eggs, separated
1/2 c. lime juice
1/4 c. water
1 tsp. lime peel, grated
green food coloring
1 c. heavy cream, whipped, plus
   extra for garnish
1 9-in. pastry shell, baked
pistachio nuts, chopped
lime slices for garnish

Thoroughly mix gelatin, 1/2 cup sugar, and salt in saucepan. Beat together egg yolks, lime juice, and water; stir into gelatin mixture. Cook and stir over medium heat until mixture just comes to a boil. Remove from heat; stir in grated peel. Add food coloring sparingly to tint pale green. Chill, stirring occasionally, until mixture mounds slightly when dropped from a spoon.

Beat egg whites until soft peaks form; gradually add 1/2 c. sugar, beating to stiff peaks. Fold gelatin mixture into egg whites. Fold in whipped cream. Pour into cooled pastry shell. Chill until firm. Spread with more whipped cream; edge with grated lime peel. Sprinkle chopped pistachio nuts in center. Garnish with lime slices placed in whipped cream mounds around edge of pie.

Ambrosia

1 1/4 c. heavy cream, whipped
2 bananas (or equivalent amount of soft fruit),
   coarsely chopped
graham crackers, broken into large crumbs

Just before serving, mix all ingredients together; pour into glasses.

Apple Crisp

1 c. brown sugar
1/2 c. all-purpose flour
1/2 tsp. nutmeg
1/2 tsp. cinnamon
1/4 tsp. salt
1/4 c. butter or margarine
5 c. tart apples, sliced (approximately 5 to 6 apples)
whipped cream or vanilla ice cream (optional)

Mix sugar, flour, spices, and salt. Cut in butter until mixture is crumbly. Spread apples in bottom of buttered 8-inch or 9-inch square baking pan. Sprinkle crumbly mixture over fruit; pat lightly with fingers. Bake, uncovered, at 350° F for 40-45 minutes or until apples are tender. Serve warm with cream or ice cream, if desired.

Danish Rice Pudding

2 c. cooked rice
2 c. low-fat milk
1/3 c. sugar
1 tsp. almond extract
1 c. heavy cream
10 oz. frozen sweetened raspberries, thawed
8 whole almonds

Heat rice, milk, and sugar in a 2-quart saucepan over medium heat, stirring frequently, until pudding is thick and creamy, about 15 minutes. Do not boil. Remove from heat; add almond extract. Cool.

Beat cream in chilled bowl until stiff peaks form. Fold whipped cream into cooled rice mixture.

Blend raspberries in blender until smooth; strain. To serve, spoon pudding into custard cups. Dollop with 1 tablespoon raspberry sauce and top with almond.

Deep-Dish Strawberry Pie

1/2 to 1 c. sugar, depending on sweetness
  of berries
1/4 c. all-purpose flour
1/8 tsp. salt
4 c. strawberries, washed and hulled
2 tbsp. butter
pastry for single-crust pie
plain or whipped cream

Combine sugar, flour, and salt. Toss lightly with berries. Fill a 1-quart baking dish with fruit mixture and dot with butter. Top with pastry which has been rolled out on pastry cloth to 1-inch larger than top of baking dish. Fold edges of pastry under and press firmly to rim of dish. Flute edges and cut gashes in pastry to allow steam to escape. Bake at 425°F for 25 minutes or until crust is browned. Serve slightly warm with plain or whipped cream.

Devil's Food Cake (microwave)

3/4 c. all-purpose flour
2/3 c. sugar
1/2 tsp. baking soda
1/2 tsp. salt
1/2 tsp. vanilla
1 oz. chocolate, melted
1/3 c. shortening
1/3 c. milk
2 eggs

Place all ingredients except eggs in mixing bowl. Blend at low speed, then beat at medium speed 1 minute. Add eggs and beat 1 minute.

If cake is to be removed before icing, place a few dabs of shortening in bottom of 9-inch, glass baking dish, then fit a circle of waxed paper over shortening.

If cake is to be iced in baking dish, simply pour batter in evenly. Cook in microwave at 50 percent power for 5-6 minutes, rotating 1/4 turn every 3 minutes. Increase power to high.

Continue cooking 2 to 5 minutes or until done. Let stand directly on countertop for 5-10 minutes.

Date Balls

1/2 c. sugar
1/2 c. brown sugar
1 pkg. dates
1 can coconut
1/2 c. butter
1 c. nuts, chopped
2 c. crisped rice cereal
powdered sugar

Combine white and brown sugars, dates, coconut, and butter. Cook 2 to 3 minutes, stirring constantly. Remove from heat; add nuts and cereal. With buttered hands, roll mixture into balls. Coat balls with powdered sugar.

Layered Banana Pudding

1/3 c. all-purpose flour
2/3 c. packed brown sugar
2 c. milk
2 egg yolks, beaten
2 tbsp. butter
1 tsp. vanilla extract
1 c. heavy cream, whipped
4 to 6 firm bananas, sliced
chopped walnuts (optional)

In a medium saucepan, combine flour and brown sugar; stir in milk. Cook over medium heat, stirring constantly, until thickened and bubbly; continue cooking and stirring 1 minute more. Remove from heat. Gradually stir about 1 cup hot mixture into egg yolks. Return all to saucepan. Bring to a gentle boil: cook and stir for 2 minutes. Remove from heat; stir in butter and vanilla. Cool to room temperature, stirring occasionally. Fold in whipped cream. Into a 2-quart glass bowl layer 1/3 pudding mixture; top with half of bananas. Repeat layers. Top with remaining pudding. Sprinkle with nuts if desired. Cover and chill at least 1 hour before serving.

Layered Banana-Pineapple Dessert

1 1/2 c. graham cracker crumbs
1/4 c. sugar
1/3 c. butter, melted
3 bananas, sliced
1 pkg. (8 oz.) cream cheese, softened
3 1/2 c. cold milk
2 pkg. (4 oz. ea.) instant vanilla pudding/pie filling
1 can (20 oz.) crushed pineapple, drained
8 oz. frozen dessert topping, thawed

Mix graham cracker crumbs, sugar, and butter in 13x9x2-inch pan. Press mixture evenly onto bottom of pan. Arrange banana slices on crust. Beat cream cheese in large bowl with wire whisk until smooth. Gradually beat in milk. Add both packages pudding mix. Beat until well blended and thickened. Spread evenly over banana slices. Spoon pineapple evenly over pudding mixture. Spread dessert topping over pineapple. Refrigerate 3 hours or until ready to serve.

Maple-Rice Pudding

1 qt. skim milk
2 c. long-grain white rice, cooked
1/3 c. plus 2 tbsp. maple syrup
1 tsp. orange rind, grated
1/2 tsp. vanilla
1/3 c. walnuts, broken

Combine milk and rice in a large saucepan. Cook, stirring constantly, over medium-low heat until mixture boils and thickens, about 25 minutes. Stir in 1/3 cup maple syrup and cook 10 minutes more. Add orange rind and vanilla. Pour into (8-ounce) dessert bowls or custard cups; allow to cool at room temperature. Meanwhile, heat walnuts in a small, heavy frying pan over low heat, stirring constantly, until fragrant, about 3 minutes. Drizzle with remaining 2 tablespoons maple syrup. Cook over medium heat, stirring, until syrup boils and coats walnuts, about 2 minutes. Sprinkle walnuts on puddings.

Index